Icon of the Revelation to John

In the Footsteps of the Saints

ST. JOHN
OF PATMOS

and the
Seven Churches
of the Apocalypse

Otto F.A. Meinardus

CARATZAS BROTHERS, PUBLISHERS
New Rochelle, New York — 1979

First published in Greece by

Lycabettus Press
P.O. Box 3391
Kolonaki
Athens
Greece

Published in North America by

CARATZAS BROTHERS, PUBLISHERS
246 Pelham Road, New Rochelle,
New.York 10805

Published in North America by

CARATZAS BROTHERS, PUBLISHERS
246 Pelham Road, New Rochelle,
New York 10805

ISBN: 0-89241-070-1 (hardcover)
ISBN: 0-89241-043-4 (paperback)
Library of Congress Catalog
Card Number 78-51245

CONTENTS

INTRODUCTION

St. John of Patmos and the Seven Churches of the Apocalypse is the third volume in the series of Biblical Holy Places in the Levant and follows the two books on *St. Paul in Greece* and *St. Paul in Ephesus and the Cities of Galatia and Cyprus*. Whereas the books on St. Paul center around the person of the Apostle, his travels, experiences, and his message to the people wherever he went, this volume reflects primarily upon the sites and churches St. John addressed in his letters. Almost half a century separates the work of St. Paul from the situations described in the following pages. The Christian communities founded by St. Paul had grown, but the initial enthusiasm was already threatened by internal dissension and heresies as well as by imperial persecution. In the last decade of the 1st century an altogether new situation had developed to which St. John, the Seer of Patmos, addressed himself.

In several ways our times, as we approach the third millenium, are not unlike those 1900 years ago. At the end of the 1st century, the Church, two or three generations old, was threatened by forces beyond its control. Several natural catastrophies had preceded the reign of the emperor Domitian and were still remembered. The consequences of the eruption of Mount Vesuvius on 23 April 79 A.D. were more far reaching than the destruction of Pompeii and Herculaneum, for the news of the catastrophe paralyzed the people all over the ancient Roman world as the ashes of the volcano were transmitted by the wind as far as Egypt and Syria. Earthquakes followed the eruption. Moreover, an ancient oracle related these disasters to the fall of Jerusalem some years earlier. The belief also prevailed that Nero, who had committed suicide in 68 A.D., had in fact fled to the East to command a Parthian army in an assault against Rome. In 80 A.D. a devastating fire swept Rome for three days and three nights, followed by a terrible plague which lasted until 81 A.D., the year the emperor Titus died to be succeeded by his brother Domitian, the first Roman emperor who insisted on being called 'God the Lord.'

Today mankind is thinking in terms of its own survival. Is there any message for today in the literature of the 1st century? Are the letters written by this ecstatic Seer on the island of Patmos relevant to people wrestling with political, economic, and social crises of world wide dimensions? Comparatively speaking, of course, few people find comfort, hope, and courage through the words of the Gospel Message, and fewer still would turn to the last book of the New Testament. The Revelation of John is probably the least seriously studied and the most misunderstood of all New Testament writings. Cranks have sadly exploited its message to fit their predetermined religious, political, or social situations, thereby robbing it of the eternal truth which shines through its pages.

This book deals with each of the three elements contained in the title: the fascinating visionary who wrote Revelation, the Aegean island of Patmos, and the Seven Churches. The Biblical name of John calls forth a wealth of associations, but the small island of Patmos is less known. The Biblical significance of Patmos, hidden for many centuries, was only rediscovered in the 11th century when a Byzantine abbot, with imperial help, established a monumental fortress-like monastery on the island and dedicated it to St. John. It was not until the 16th century that Western pilgrims repaired to the island, and the recent scholarly interest in Patmos has centered around its famous library treasures rather than the sites hallowed by the presence of St. John.

The stories of the Seven Churches in Asia Minor are testimonies to faith and unbelief, to steadfastness and surrender. While the Early Church was aware of the Biblical significance of the Seven Churches, in the later days of the Byzantine Empire and during the Ottoman period their

ii

apostolic association was less remembered. Some of the churches were abandoned, and their sites were rediscovered only in the middle of the 17th century. The Reverend Thomas Smith, British chaplain at Constantinople and later at Smyrna, pointed out that "the English gentlemen who live in Smyrna, out of a pious zeal and a justly commendable curiosity, were the first who made a voyage thither to see the remainders of that magnificence, for which those cities were so renowned in the histories of ancient times." In April 1671 Smith, in a party of twelve, including two Armenians, set out from Smyrna to visit the remaining six churches and to provide us with the first account of the state of these sites. A few years later Sir Paul Rycaut, British consul at Smyrna, accompanied by the Reverend Dr. John Luke, chaplain to the factory in Smyrna, followed in the steps of Smith's party. Rycaut and Luke identified the almost forgotten sites of Thyatira and Laodicea, the former having become the Turkish town of Akhisar, the latter only ruins. The Reverend Edmund Chishull, chaplain at Smyrna in 1698, visited Ephesus, Sardis, and Thyatira. In the beginning of the 19th century, the Reverend H. Lindsay, British chaplain at Constantinople, visited the Seven Churches. A few years later the Reverend Francis Vyvian J. Arundell, chaplain at Smyrna from 1821-1840, wrote the first scholarly account of the archaeology and history of the Seven Churches. Other 19th century travelers included H. Christmas and A.S. Noroff, though it was not until the early 20th century that Sir William M. Ramsay investigated the archaeology of these former churches which he published in his *The Letters to the Seven Churches of Asia*. The ecclesiastical situation and the spiritual strength of these Seven Churches before the First World War were ably described and analysed by George Lambakis, private secretary to Queen Olga, in his study *The Seven Stars of the Apocalypse* (in Greek). In 1963 the Reverend Vernon P. Flynn, pastor of the Dutch Chapel in Istanbul, published a series of sermons entitled *The Seven Churches Today*.

As tourism to the archaeological sites in Greece and

Turkey has increased, so has the number of travelers wishing to know about the history and archaeology of the Seven Churches. Unfortunately, none of the above mentioned accounts are readily available to most tourists, for most are out of print. We sincerely hope, therefore, that the following pages will be a helpful introduction to the historically interested Bible student and traveler.

None of the earlier descriptions of the Seven Churches included information about the island of Patmos, which was reached only with difficulty until the early 20th century. Even today it is difficult to combine a journey to Patmos and the Seven Churches, because from Patmos the Turkish mainland can only be reached via the islands of Cos and Rhodes to the south or Samos and Chios to the north. Ephesus, well known for its outstanding ruins, attracts an increasing number of visitors each year. Some material included in *St. Paul in Ephesus* is contained in the Ephesus chapter of this volume. Smyrna, the modern city of Izmir, is the largest and most important city and port of the eastern Aegean. While the classical and Biblical Pergamum is in ruins, the modern Bergama at the foot of the acropolis and south of the Selinos River is the chief town of a district. The ruins of the temples of the acropolis and the asklepium bring more and more visitors to this town every year. The carpet making center of Akhisar, the former Thyatira, is a prosperous modern town with few significant remains of its ancient glory. Near the extensive ruins of ancient Sardis is the little village of Sartmustafa, a sad survival of the former Lydian capital. Alashehir, the former Philadelphia, is a growing town in the fertile valley at the foot of the Tmolous Mountains or Boz Dagi. With some remaining Byzantine walls and winding streets, Alashehir is one of the more picturesque towns of the region. Finally, there are the deserted ruins of Laodicea between Pamukkale and Denizli.

In the summer of 1973 I revisited the island of Patmos and the Seven Churches, traveling by public transport from Izmir (Smyrna) to Bergama (Pergamum) and from there via Soma to Akhisar (Thyatira). There I took the minibus to

Manisa (Magnesia) where I visited the Archaeological Museum with its treasures from Thyatira and Sardis. My next stop was Sartmustafa (Sardis), on the main highway from Manisa a few miles west of Salihli. From Salihli I proceeded to Alashehir (Philadelphia) and then to Sarigol. Travelers using public transport should remember that no regular bus or minibus services are available from Sarigol across the high mountain range of Boz Dagi to Saraykoy and Denizli. Laodicea can be reached from Denizli by taking a minibus to Eskihisar. Regular bus services connect Denizli with Selçuk, from which the ruins of Ephesus are easily accessible. With private transport the sites of the Seven Churches can be visited easily within two or three days.

In the description of the present sites of Patmos and the Seven Churches I have limited myself to the Christian monuments and remains. The archaeology and history of temples, public buildings, etc. can be easily located in any reputable guide book. Throughout the following pages I have used the ancient Greek or Biblical geographical names for the period before the Ottoman era and the Turkish names thereafter.

The dates in parentheses after the names of Christian saints signify the days and months of the saints' martyrdoms, as commemorated by the Orthodox Church. A list of the 15th to 19th century travelers consulted appears at the end of this volume. All quotations from the Holy Scriptures are from the Revised Standard Version of the Bible, copyrighted in 1946 and 1952 by the Division of Christian Education of the National Council of Churches of Christ in the U.S.A., and are used by permission. I should like to acknowledge the encouragement and advice received from my colleagues of the American School of Classical Studies in Athens and the American Collegiate Institute in Izmir. Finally, I want to express my gratitude to my secretary, Mrs. Sophia Hanazoglu, for preparing the manuscript for publication.

St. Andrew's American Church   Otto F. A. Meinardus
Athens, Greece, 1974

ST. JOHN OF PATMOS

The Author of the Seven Letters

Who was this John, the author of "The revelation of Jesus Christ, which God gave him to show to his servants what must soon take place?" He refers to himself as Christ's servant (Rev. 1:1) and calls himself a brother of those to whom he is writing (Rev. 1:9). Apparently, there is little distinction between the author and the people he addresses. We infer that he was a Christian confessor who testified to his faith before the Roman authorities and was exiled to Patmos, where he suffered tribulation and with patient endurance waited for the kingdom (Rev. 1:9). He claimed to be a prophet (Rev. 1:3) writing with the authority of divine inspiration (Rev. 22:18). From his writing we can deduce that he knew at least some Hebrew, which suggests that he was a Jewish Christian, probably of the diaspora. He knew the Old Testament well, though he seldom quoted it. He also knew the Pauline corpus of letters, which may have inspired him to write the letters to the Seven Churches.

John lived when emperor worship was the predominant religion, for it insured the loyalty to Rome of the heterogeneous people living around the "Roman lake" of the Mediterranean. Christians refused to participate in this worship, which required citizens to take an oath by the divine spirit of the emperor and to offer incense and wine in honor of the emperor's godhead on the altar before his image. To the Roman administrative officials this refusal signified disloyalty and rebellion. Official suspicion was increased because the

17th Century Icon of St. John Dictating the Fourth Gospel to Prochorus
The Byzantine Museum, Athens

1

Christians used to meet secretly, either during the night or at daybreak.

A contemporary description of the official perplexity concerning the behavior of the Christians of Asia Minor is contained in a letter written by Pliny the Younger, governor of Bithynia, to the emperor Trajan between 111 and 113.

> It is my custom, my lord, to refer to you all questions about which I have doubts. I have no little uncertainty whether pardon is granted on repentance, or whether when one has been a Christian there is no gain to him in that he has ceased to be such; whether the mere name, without crimes, or crimes connected with the name are punished. Those who were accused before me as Christians asserted that the amount of their fault or error was this: That they had been accustomed to assemble on a fixed day before daylight and sing by turns a hymn to Christ as a god; and that they bound themselves with an oath, not for any crime, but to commit neither theft, nor robbery, nor to break their word and not deny a deposit when demanded; after these things were done, it was their custom to depart and meet together again to take food, but ordinary and harmless food; and they said even this had ceased after my edict was issued, by which, according to your commands, I had forbidden the existence of clubs. On this account I believed it the more necessary to find out from two maid-servants, who were called deaconesses, and that by torture, what was the truth. I found nothing else than a perverse and excessive superstition. I therefore adjourned the examination and hastened to consult you. The matter seemed to me to be worth deliberation.

When he found Christians who persisted three times over in saying that they were Christians, he ordered them to be executed. Others, including some who admitted that they had been Christians, when questioned, cursed Christ and worshiped the statues of the gods and that of the emperor, things which, according to Pliny, those who are "really Christians" would not do.

It was in this political climate that St. John was exiled to the island of Patmos, off the coast of Asia Minor and about sixty miles southwest of Ephesus. Banishment to one of the small rocky islands of the Aegean was a common and recognized penalty, which carried with it not only loss of civil rights but also the entire loss of property. The emperor Domitian banished his niece Flavia Domitilla to a small island called Pontia and executed her husband, apparently because they had been attracted to the new faith. Pliny the Elder mentions that Patmos occasionally was used as a place of banishment. The penalty normally lasted as long as the exile's life. Usually he was allowed to move freely among the islanders, but in some cases he was put to forced labor. Many Christians were punished in this manner. In its worst forms banishment was a terrible fate since it was accompanied by fetters, scanty clothing, insufficient food, sleep on the bare ground in a dark prison, and work under the lash of military overseers. We do not know the "tribulation" St. John referred to, whether he meant the persecution to which all of Asia was exposed or some particular suffering on the island of Patmos.

It always had been dangerous to be a Christian. The Roman authorities had listed the cults that might be practised in the empire, but Christianity was not one of them. Ever since the days of Jesus Christ, Christian spokesmen such as Stephen, James, Peter, and Paul had suffered martyrdom, and in order to survive the Christians had to disguise themselves. By the end of the 1st century emperor worship was demanded from all, and it was at this point that St. John, the Seer of Patmos, proclaimed his clear message of "no compromise" to the Christians of the Seven Churches in the Roman province of Asia: Ephesus, Smyrna, Pergamum, Thyatira, Sardis, Philadelphia, and Laodicea.

The late 1st century persecutions under the Flavian emperors in Asia Minor as reflected in the Book of Revelation were an organized attempt to exterminate Christianity, much

3

more than the sporadic though stern repressions which occurred during the 2nd century. They stopped, however, in 96 when Domitian was assassinated by Stephanus, the freedman of Domitian's banished and widowed niece Domitilla, and the Christians profited greatly from the subsequent annulling of all Domitian's acts. Though not instituted by Domitian, the persecutions have been closely connected with his name and his ideas. Apparently the sentence against St. John was ordered by him, and was lifted when all his acts were annulled.

Traditions about St. John

Shortly after the middle of the 2nd century Justin Martyr, who had visited Ephesus in 135, stated that the Revelation was written by "John, one of the apostles of Christ." This opinion came to be widely accepted in the Early Church and still has its supporters. Despite the observation by Papias, the 2nd century bishop of Hierapolis, that "the statement of those is true, who assert that there were two of the same name in Asia, and that there were also two tombs in Ephesus, and that both are called John's even to this day, which is particularly necessary to observe," Christian tradition has uncritically settled for one person named John, the son of Zebedee, the brother of James, the beloved disciple and apostle, the evangelist and theologian, the elder and the seer of Patmos.

Our task is neither to disentangle the various personalities whom tradition has joined into one person nor to record all the Johannine traditions which have been assembled. We shall limit ourselves to a selection of stories pertaining to St. John's exile on Patmos and his ministry in Ephesus. The principal non-Biblical sources are the apocryphal Acts of John and the Travels and Miracles of

St. John the Theologian, Apostle and Evangelist, traditionally set down by his disciple Prochorus.

Tradition is consistent that St. John came to Ephesus, where he wrote the Gospel as well as the three general epistles. Some sources claim that he was accompanied by Mary, the Mother of Our Lord, in response to the statement made by Jesus Christ on the Cross.

> When Jesus saw his mother, and the disciple whom he loved standing near, he said to his mother, "Woman, behold your son!" And from that hour the disciple took her to his own home.
>
> John 19:26, 27.

Others hold that St. John arrived in Ephesus after the dormition of the Holy Virgin in 67.

St. John Saves a Young Man from Drowning
17th century wall painting from the Monastery of St. John (Exonarthex), Patmos

5

When Domitian (81-96 A.D.) became emperor, he began persecuting the Jews, who transferred government displeasure to the Christian brethren throughout Asia Minor. John, the head of the church in Ephesus, was arrested by the Romans, but instead of being crucified as was his Master, he was exiled to Patmos with his disciple, Prochorus, one of the deacons of the Jerusalem church (Acts 6:5).

The ship carrying the exiles was caught in a violent storm in the Aegean Sea, and a large wave swept one of the passengers into the water. The victim's father, in a state of utter frenzy, was about to throw himself into the waves after his son when the other passengers turned to the Apostle for help. St. John raised his hands to heaven and implored the name of the one true God. With his chained hands he made the sign of the cross, and the sea returned the lost man alive. The storm calmed and the crew and passengers expressed their joy to the Apostle, who then transformed the deck into a pulpit to proclaim the message of salvation. When the ship arrived at the island the Apostle was delivered to Laurentius, the Roman governor of Patmos, who freed him of his chains. Laurentius's father-in-law, Myron, offered the Apostle lodging in his house, and soon Myron's house became the first church on the island. Apollonides, Myron's son, who was possessed by the devil, was healed by St. John, and this miracle led to the conversion of both Chrysippe, Myron's daughter, and her husband, the Roman governor. The remains of St. John's traditional baptismal font are enclosed by a metal fence near the Chapel of St. John in Skala.

When the priests of the Temple of Apollo in Patmos learned that St. John was converting the leading citizens to the new faith, they asked Kynops, a famous magician on the island, to end the Apostle's influence. Before a great crowd of Patmians, Kynops challenged St. John with a display of his magical powers. He ended by jumping into the sea, from

St. John's Traditional Baptismal Font near the Chapel of St. John in Skala, Patmos

which he intended to reappear as he had done on several former occasions. The Apostle, however, extending his arms in the form of a cross, exclaimed: "O Thou, who didst grant to Moses by this similitude to overthrow Amalek, O Lord Jesus Christ, bring down Kynops to the deep of the sea; let him never more behold this sun, nor converse with living men." As the Apostle spoke, the sea roared and the water formed a whirlpool where Kynops went down. Kynops sank to the bottom and did not reappear. A Patmian tradition identifies a submerged rock in the harbor of Skala, 300 m. from the dock and marked by a white buoy, as petrified Kynops. The Patmian fishermen say that the octopodes caught by this rock are inedible, because Kynops's wickedness spoiled their taste. The name of the magician is also still attached to one of the southern promontories of Patmos, Ghenoupas, a wild and precipitous area in which a cave is said to have been his dwelling place.

A few miles southeast of Chora, on the way to Grikou, is the white Chapel of St. John the Theologian at Sykamia. A local tradition, faithfully upheld, maintains that here St. John baptized and healed the islanders and also delivered them from a man-eating monster.

When the people of Patmos, converted by St. John, found that he was about to leave them, they begged him to write them a narrative of the miracles he had seen concerning the Son of God, and of His words which he had heard, that they might remain steadfast in their faith. St. John's disciple Prochorus then narrates how he went with the Apostle to a tranquil spot by a low hill a mile distant from the city. After long fasting and prayer, the Apostle had Prochorus sit nearby with paper and ink and, then, standing and looking up steadfastly into heaven, he dictated to Prochorus the Gospel, starting "In the beginning was the Word" (John 1:1).

The holy grotto between the port of Skala and the

St. John Condemns Kynops to the Waves
17th century wall painting from the Monastery of St. John (Exonarthex), Patmos

monastery, which some tradition identifies also as the site of the writing of the Fourth Gospel, is the site of the writing of the Revelation. The 12th century *Byzantine Guide to Painting* by the monk Dionysius which, from the early Middle Ages until today has determined the depiction of sacred subjects in the art of the Orthodox Church, offers the following directions: For the writing of the Gospel, "St. John the Evangelist is seated in a grotto in ecstasy. He turns his head backwards towards heaven; his right hand rests upon his knee, the left is extended towards St. Prochorus who is seated before St. John." For the writing of the Revelation, "St. John the Theologian is seated in a grotto, he looks behind him and is wrapped in ecstasy. He sees Christ seated on the clouds, clothed with a white garment, and girt with a golden girdle; He has in His right hand seven stars, and out of His mouth comes a sharp edged sword. Several golden lamps surround Him, and a great radiance issues from his person."

Traditions have assigned various lengths to St. John's exile on Patmos. Most sources refer to a period of 18 months. St. Irenaeus, the 2nd century bishop of Lyons, mentions five years and the anonymous author of the 7th century *Chronicon Paschale* mentions fifteen years. St. Victorinus of Pettau even suggested that St. John was sent to work in the mines on Patmos. After the death of Domitian and his release from exile, St. John returned to Ephesus and, according to the 4th century church historian, Eusebius, "governed the churches in Asia." Irenaeus wrote that "all the elders of Asia had conferred with John the disciple of our Lord, and that he continued with them until the time of Trajan (98-117)." Clement of Alexandria (2nd century) wrote that St. John appointed bishops and established entire new congregations in the neigboring regions of Ephesus. One day, while visiting one of those newly established churches, he committed to the care of a bishop "a youth of fine stature, graceful countenance, and ardent mind." The bishop educated and finally baptized the youth. After this, however, the bishop relaxed his care and vigilance. The youth fell away from the church and eventually became the captain of a band of

10

robbers. When St. John returned to this particular church and asked the bishop about the youth he had entrusted to his care, the bishop replied, "He is dead to God." On hearing this, the aged Apostle rode into the country to meet the youth and restored his faith.

While the state threatened the church from the outside, heresies undermined its stability and unity from the inside. Eusebius relates that one day the Apostle John entered the bath in Ephesus and saw Cerinthus the heretic, whereupon the Apostle leapt up and fled, not enduring to remain under the same roof with him, and he exhorted those with him to do the same, saying, "let us flee, lest the bath fall in, as long as Cerinthus, that enemy of the truth, is within."

About the death of St. John we know little. The Early Church maintained that "John, who rested on the bosom of our Lord, who was a priest that bore the sacerdotal plate (Ex. 38:36, 39:30), and martyr and teacher, he also rests at Ephesus."

Chapel of St. John at Sykamia, Patmos

THE ISLAND OF PATMOS

Historical Outline

Patmos, 10 miles long and 6 miles wide, is one of the smallest Aegean islands. It is volcanic, bare, and rocky. Were it not for the enforced exile of St. John and the acceptance of his Revelation in the canon of Holy Scripture, the island would have remained only one of the many islands off the coast of Asia Minor. Its association with Biblical history however, has converted Patmos to a Christian holy place.

Little is known about the early history of Patmos. Mycenaean and Geometric period potsherds bear witness to its habitation from the 14th - 8th century B.C. Archaeological research has confirmed the existence of Artemis and Apollo cults on the island. The island is mentioned in the 5th century B.C. by Thucydides and in the 1st century B.C. by Strabo. As we know from the experience of St. John, the Roman authorities used it as a place of banishment. From the 7th - 11th century the island seems to have been deserted because of incursions by Arab pirates. An early 10th century account by an imprisoned bishop refers to Patmos as an island where "we had to endure most grievous trials, for the place was arid, and thirst afflicted the prisoners." In 1088 the Blessed Christodoulus founded the famous Monastery of St. John the Theologian near the port of Nestia, but, warned by a vision, he moved the monastery to the second highest point of the island and fortified it.

Christodoulus (March 16) was born in 1020 in Nicaea, the modern Iznik, in the province of Bithynia. He embraced the anchoritic life at Mount Olympus near Bursa, and later lived

The Monastery of the Apocalypse (foreground) and the Monastery of St. John, Patmos as a hermit in the wilderness of Judaea. The patriarch Nicholas III of Constantinople (1084-1111) ordained him archimandrite and placed him in charge of twenty monasteries on Mount Latmus near Miletus. These monasteries were successively devastated by the Selçuk Turks, so he decided to build a monastery on Patmos. He was given financial aid by the emperor Alexius I Comnenus, who advised the abbot to allow a few lay families to settle on the island to lessen the severity of the monastic life. Christodoulus died on the island of Euboea in 1093. After some time, his relics were translated from Euboea to Patmos, where they soon acquired the reputation of working miraculous cures. The feast of the translation of his relics is celebrated on October 21.

The monastery soon became the most significant religious, cultural, and intellectual center in the Aegean Sea, largely because of the financial support given by the Byzantine emperors and patriarchs. The monks became the masters of Patmos with "the right to be absolute rulers to all eternity" according to an imperial grant. Though frequently threatened by pirates, lack of personnel, and interferences by neighboring administrators and bishops, the monastery survived thoughout the centuries. In 1207 the Venetians seized the island from the Byzantines. After the fall of Constantinople to the Ottoman Turks in 1453, Pope Pius II in 1461 and Pope Leo X in 1513 extended their protection to the island and the monastery. In 1537 Patmos was occupied by the Turks, to whom the monks paid an annual tribute. In general, however, Patmos thrived under the Ottoman administration. The prestige of the monastery and its favorable relations with the papacy in Rome and the Knights of St. John of Malta enabled the Patmian fleet, flying the flag of the Knights, to sail unhindered throughout the Mediterranean and Black Sea. The monastery increased in wealth and prestige as it acquired properties on many Aegean islands — Samos, Paros, Milos, Naxos, Siphnos, Icaria, Amorgos— and Zakinthos in the Ionian Sea. In 1695 the Venetians under Francesco Morosini carried out a savage raid

14

on the island and plundered Chora. Its effects were so devastating that the island's prosperous maritime trade was annihilated, and it took years to recover from the blow. A monk drew the battle, showing ships of all shapes and sizes, on the walls of the Chapel of St. Basil in the Monastery of St. John the Theologian. Some of the ships are shown without rigging, with sails furled, or at anchor, indicating that they were taken by surprise while lying in harbor.

Despite this Venetian success the island remained Turkish until 1821, when it gained temporary independence, thanks to the courage of such Patmians as Emmanuel Xanthos and Demetrios Themelis. The Treaty of Constantinople in 1832, however, returned the island to the Turks. In 1912 Patmos was annexed by Italy and only became a formal part of the Greek state after the Second World War, according to the terms of the Treaty of Paris in 1947.

The Monastery of the Apocalypse

The island is divided into two nearly equal sections by an isthmus where the ancient town was situated. The modern town, Skala, has grown from a tiny port into the financial and tourist center of the island. From Skala the road ascends to the Monastery of the Apocalypse enshrining the Grotto of the Revelation. North of the grotto Christodoulus built the 11th century Chapel of St. Anna in honor of both the Holy Virgin's mother and the mother of Alexius I Comnenus. When M. de Tournefort visited the grotto in 1702 it was a poor hermitage, which had been given by the abbot of St. John's Monastery to the bishop of Samos. The abbot gave the traveler some pieces of rock from the grotto, assuring him that they could expel evil spirits and cure diseases. A few years later the grotto reverted to the Patmians, for when Richard Pococke came to the island in 1739, the grotto was "a sort of novitiate or seminary subject to the great monastery."

In 1713 the Patmias School was founded by Makarios Kalogheras in the buildings of the Monastery of the Apocalypse. This school soon acquired an excellent reputation, for when Basil Gregory Barsky, a monk from Kiev, visited Patmos in 1731, he wrote, "For the Greeks who are under Turkish yoke, this school undertook the significance of ancient Athens." In the neighboring islands Patmos was known as the "University of the Archipelago," and the Greek families sent their sons to study here. In the middle of the 19th century the school was abandoned, largely because of competition from schools that had sprung up elsewhere. The new Patmias School was built after the Second World War and includes a theological seminary.

Near the grotto, in addition to the Chapel of St. Anna, are the two chapels of St. Nicholas and St. Artemius. For a description of the holy grotto we quote the present abbot of the Monastery of St. John the Theologian, Archimandrite Theodoritos Bournis:

> To the right of the Church of St. Anna we see the dreadful Grotto, where John saw and wrote his Revelation. Filled with awe, we approach this Holy Rock. We distinguish a small conch chiselled out of the rock. The Great Visualizer used to rest his head there. Above the conch we perceive a hewn cross which is traced back to St. John's holy hands. To the right we see a chiselled grip which served as a prop to St. John, when he wanted to kneel down in order to pray or to get up. To the right and above the grip, one sees a rocky bookstand where Prochorus wrote the Revelation at his teacher's dictation. Most thrilling is the dreadful cleft in the rock. It stretches from south to north, above the place where St. John rested, and divides the rock into three parts. This rock was shaped when St. John heard God's voice saying: "I am the Alpha and the Omega."

The most significant icon in the grotto represents the Revelation of St. John, and shows Christ appearing to St. John as the Apostle lies at His feet in a trance (frontispiece). In the

16

upper part of the icon Christ is shown enthroned; "clothed with a long robe and with a golden girdle round his breast, His eyes are like a flame of fire, His feet like burnished bronze" (Rev. 1:13-15). In His right hand He holds seven stars and in His left hand the keys of Death and Hades. From His mouth issues a sharp two-edged sword. Around Christ are seven angels holding in their hands seven churches, and seven candlesticks stand in front of Him.

The Grotto of the Apocalypse, Patmos

The Monastery of St. John the Theologian

Just beyond the Monastery of the Apocalypse are the buildings of the new Patmias School. By following either the donkey path or the main road the visitor will soon reach the village of Chora with the monastery fortress of St. John the Theologian, one of the most impressive monasteries in the eastern Mediterranean.

The main church of St. John the Theologian is immediately to the left of the central courtyard. The exonarthex is adorned with 17th - 19th century wall paintings, of which the oldest and best preserved depict scenes from the apocryphal Life of St. John. From left to right they show the miracle of the raising of young Domnus in Ephesus, St. John saving the youth who had fallen overboard on the journey from Ephesus to Patmos, the death of the magician Kynops in Patmos and, on the south wall, the falling asleep of St. John. The right or southern door of the exonarthex leads to the small Chapel of the Blessed Christodoulus, where his relics repose in a wooden casket set in a marble sarcophagus. The 18th century silver gilt ornamentations are the work of a silversmith of Smyrna.

The narthex of the main church is adorned with early 19th century wall paintings depicting New Testament scenes. Noteworthy here is the large 11th century icon of St. John holding the Fourth Gospel. In the sanctuary, also adorned with 17th - 19th century wall paintings, are a number of valuable icons. A large icon of the Revelation of St. John on the north wall hides the entrance to the small 17th century treasury built by Bishop Nicephoros of Laodicea. East of the sanctuary is the ancient treasury, containing one of the largest reliquaries of the Eastern Church, including parts of the skulls of the Apostle Thomas and St. Antipas of Pergamum, and parts of St. Philip the Deacon, St. Titus, and St. Timothy. The 12th century chapel to the south of the main sanctuary adorned with 13th century frescos is dedicated to the Holy Virgin. These paintings, together with those in the 11th century barrel vaulted refectory southeast of the main church, are the oldest in the monastery.

Since its founding the Monastery of St. John has been famous for its library, with almost 900 manuscripts and more than 2,000 old printed books. The oldest text is the purple parchment, Codex 67, an early 6th century fragment of the Gospel of St. Mark. This fragment consists of 33 leaves, and additional parts of this manuscript are in the libraries in Leningrad, Vienna, the British Museum, the Vatican, and the Byzantine Museum in Athens. Among the other ancient and valuable manuscripts are Codex 171, an 8th century text of Job, and the 10th century Codex 33 containing the discourses of St. Gregory the Theologian. The monastery's treasury, with its exquisite collection of icons, chalices, vestments, and embroideries, is one of the finest Byzantine art collections in the world, with gifts from Russia, Moldavia, Wallachia, Mount Athos, and Italy.

The Monastery of St. John the Theologian is *idiorrhythmic,* meaning that each monk retains his personal property, eats his meals in his own cell, and determines the degree of his own ascetic practices. The monastery is a patriarchal establishment and is subject to the Greek Orthodox Patriarchate of Constantinople. The monastic fellowship counts among its distinguished members H. B. Athenagoras, Archbishop of Thyatira and Great Britain, and H. B. John, Bishop of Helsinki, Finland.

Travelers to Patmos

From the 16th century onwards, Western travelers have been attracted to Patmos. When Reinhold Lubenau arrived at the harbor of Patmos in 1589, then known as Porto Domitiano, he was greeted by monks who were called "Johanniti de patina." In the monastery he was shown the hand of St. John with which the Gospel and the Revelation were written, and he was told that the nails continue growing on the fingers of this hand, requiring regular clipping. Twenty years later Sandys visited the island. It seems that at this time the monks were in charge of the shipmasters and tradesmen, since in the 17th century the island had commercial relations with many cities in Asia Minor, Russia, Egypt, and Cyprus. Joseph Georgirenes, Archbishop of Samos, wrote an account of Patmos in 1677. In the deserted village of Phocas he saw among the ruins a church,

> which they say was built in St. John's days and they show something like a pulpit. . . . Besides the port of Diacopti is a steep rock of a very great height which is called Kynops. Here Kynops the magician was believed to have lodged in a great cave which they believe to be haunted by devils. For once for curiosity's sake they let down a man by rope to see what was in the cave, but when they pulled him up he was dead!

Pitton de Tournefort, visiting the island in 1702, was astounded by the bells in the monastery. Upon inquiry he was told that the Turks also venerated St. John as a prophet and therefore allowed the monks to use the bells. At this time the monastery had about 100 monks, though no more than 60 lived in the monastery itself. In terms of the civilian population, Tournefort estimated that there were barely 300 men on Patmos, with one man to at least twenty women, "who are naturally pretty, but disfigure themselves so with paint, that they are really frightful, yet that is far from their intention." He was told that there were 250 chapels on the island though only 10 priests, "the plague having swept away the others." There were neither Turks nor Franks on Patmos.

By 1739 the number of monks had increased to 200, of whom 20 were priests. In that year Richard Pococke estimated that Chora included some 700 houses, though only 160 persons payed the poll tax. The prosperity of the island in general and of the monastery in particular may have been partly the result of the protection the Hapsburg emperor Charles VI extended in 1727 against the constant threats by pirates.

In the 19th century the fame of the monastery library began to attract Western bibliophiles interested in acquiring manuscripts for the critical study of the Scriptures and the Classics. The abbot, aware of the treasures and the temptations of his monks to sell manuscripts, had the following text posted above the door of the library:

> In this place are lying whatever manuscripts there are of note, more estimable are they to a wise man than gold: Guard them, therefore, watchfully, more than your life; for on their account is this Monastery now become conspicious. In the month of August 1802.

In 1810 Edward D. Clarke visited the library and "found it to be nearly filled with books of all sizes in a most neglected state." He took some of the most valuable manuscripts with him to England. Nonetheless, Konstantin von Tischendorf remarked almost 40 years later that "this library is indisputably one of the richest in the East," and von Tischendorf had examined almost all monastic libraries in the Christian Orient. Von Tischendorf was also shown two dark rocks, of which one was said to be a disobedient daughter turned by her mother's curse into stone, and the other a false prophet, transformed by the convincing eye of St. John. According to C.T. Newton, British vice consul in Mytilene in the middle of the 19th century, the titular ruler of Patmos was an Ottoman *mudir* who, however, did not reside on the island. In practice, the island was ruled by a *demarchia*, a corporation of three or four of the wealthiest Greeks who, "being the richest are said to be the most dishonest."

Almost all travelers have commented upon the unique panorama visible from the roof of the Monastery of St. John. In the. northwest is the low level line of the island of Icaria, further north are the peaks of Samos and the promontory of Mycale, to the southeast is the island of Leros, beyond which rise the five summits of the island of Kalymnos. To the southwest lies the island of Amorgos and the distant volcanic island of Santorini or Thera. The sea is studded with numerous islets, and these, together with the intervening spaces of deep blue water, give the basic structure to the scene.

This was the view which, with frequent changes from sunshine to storm, must have impressed St. John. Some travelers have pointed out that the impression this scene made upon him is reflected in the imagery of the Revelation when he writes that "the sky vanished like a scroll that is rolled up, and every mountain and island was removed from its place" (Rev. 6:14), or that "every island fled away, and no mountains were to be found; and great hailstones, heavy as a hundred-weight, dropped on men from heaven" (Rev. 16:20, 21). Theodore Bent, writing in 1888, went one step further and suggested that the Revelation was written under the actual influence of an eruption of the volcano on the island of Thera, which he identified with the "beast rising out of the sea" (Rev. 13:1).

THE SEVEN CHURCHES OF ASIA

Historical Outline

The Seven Churches addressed by St. John in the 2nd and 3rd chapters of his Revelation are in western Turkey, and their fortunes and trials are intimately linked to the history of this part of Asia Minor.

In Asia Minor the great Hittite civilization (ca. 1850 - 1200 B.C.) was followed by the Phrygian period (ca. 1200 - 700 B.C.). The Greek colonization of western Asia Minor began toward the end of the Phrygian period, and the history of the area from ca. 700 to 546 B.C. is of the indigenous city states such as Caria, Lycia, and Lydia and their relations with the new Greek colonies such as Ephesus, Miletus, and Sardis. The Lydians, under their fabled King Croesus, became the most powerful state in the area until Cyrus the Great of Persia defeated Croesus in 546 B.C. and brought most of Asia Minor under Persian control.

Persian predominance in Asia Minor lasted until Alexander the Great pushed his astonishing campaign across the Hellespont in 334 B.C. Alexander's advance brought Greek culture to the fore, where it remained for almost 1800 years. Alexander's immediate successor in Asia Minor was Lysimachus, one of Alexander's generals, who gained control of Lydia, Mysia, and most of the Greek cities. Lysimachus was defeated in 281 B.C. and his territory fell to the Seleucid kingdom. The Hellenistic city of Pergamum, which gained its independence by this Seleucid victory, eventually contributed much to Seleucid defeat. Pergamum grew to be a powerful city; it was Pergamum which stopped the Galatians in 230 B.C. As an ally of Rome, Pergamum gave decisive assistance in the battle of Magnesia in 190 B.C. in which the Roman general Scipio Africanus defeated Antiochus III, ending the Seleucid kingdom in Asia Minor. Rome was predominant in the area from this period on. After 133 B.C., when Attalus III of Pergamum bequeathed his kingdom to Rome, the area with which we are concerned came under direct Roman rule, becoming part of the Roman province of Asia in 129 B.C.

The Roman presence in Asia Minor, however, did not advance unopposed. Roman rule in Asia Minor was bought at great cost, against which the later Roman concern with political loyalty expressed in the state religion is understandable. The main fount of dissension was the kingdom of Pontus, in northeastern Asia Minor, which came under the rule of the extraordinary Mithradates VI in ca. 111 B.C. Mithradates began effective resistance to Roman rule shortly after the turn of the century and continued almost without interruption for the next forty years.

In 92 B.C. a Roman army under Sulla cleared Cappadocia of Mithradates' supporters, but in 88 B.C. Mithradates overran the Roman province of Asia and declared an anti-Roman crusade, in response to which approximately 100,000 Romans in the province were murdered. Sulla returned with another Roman army in 87 B.C., drove the Pontic forces from the area, and concluded a peace with Mithradates in 85 B.C., but the devastation wrought by this conflict was terrible. In 74 B.C. Mithradates again marched against Roman forces, occupying the new Roman province of Bithynia and defeating the Romans at Chalcedon. The Romans rallied under Lucullus and halted Mithradates' advance, destroying his army in the following two years. Mithradates himself escaped, and in 69 B.C. was back in Pontus harrassing the Roman occupying forces. Mithradates was finally curbed only when the Roman senate concentrated enough power in the hands of Pompey to stamp out the powerful pirates of the eastern Mediterranean, and Pompey then moved on against the now isolated but still dangerous

The Cities of Western Asia Minor
⊗ The Seven Churches of the Apocalypse

Mithradates. Mithradates escaped again, this time across the Caucasus to the Crimea where in 63 B.C. he finally died, in his late sixties, planning an invasion of Italy.

Although Roman rule was now firmly entrenched, the central authority was repeatedly overturned by provincial Roman officials. In the fifty years before Diocletian (284 - 305 A.D.) there were approximately twenty emperors, each of whom ruled an average of two and a half years. In 297 A.D. Diocletian reduced this threat by breaking up the large provinces, giving to many of the new provinces thus formed their ancient regional names. The province of Asia was broken into six new provinces.

The importance of the eastern lands to the Roman Empire was underscored by the construction of the new Roman capital in Byzantium by Constantine the Great in 330 A.D. In the early years of what became known as the Byzantine Empire, Asia Minor was subjected to major invasions by Germanic tribes who ravaged the Balkans and Asia Minor as their Galatian predecessors had done in the 3rd century B.C. The Byzantines, nonetheless, maintained their empire throughout the eastern Mediterranean until the 7th century, when a short lived Persian success and the later explosion of Islam drove them back into Anatolia. The Persian and later Arab successes slashed into Asia Minor, and the emperor Heraclius divided the area into large military zones known as *themes;* the *theme* containing the Seven Churches was Thracesion.

Despite their successes elsewhere, the Arabs were never able to retain control over Asia Minor, and the Byzantine heartland was not long occupied by hostile forces until the arrival of the Turks. The major Turkish advance into Asia Minor was marked by the Selçuk victory at Mantzikert in 1071; most of the imperial army, including the emperor Romanus Diogenes, was killed. Within a few years the Selçuk Turks controlled large areas in Asia Minor and had settled in Iconium as their capital. The Selçuks were replaced by the Ottoman Turks in the 14th century, and before the inexorable Turkish advance the Byzantine Empire slowly declined. The situation was complicated by the Crusades, particularly the Fourth Crusade which captured Constantinople in 1204 and settled a number of Latin kingdoms in what had been Byzantine territory. Early in the 15th century Tamerlane swept through Asia Minor, decimating all opposition and throwing the Ottoman Empire into a war of succession which lasted 20 years. Despite these interruptions, the Ottoman Turks were in control of virtually all the territory of the Seven Churches by the end of the 14th century. In 1453 the Ottomans finally captured Constantinople, making it their capital.

Although Ottoman rule removed Christianity from its predominant position, some of the Seven Churches continued to exist in their now subservient role. Some of them, such as Smyrna, flourished and grew as its Greek community prospered, but the others gradually weakened or disappeared completely. The upheaval for all the Christian communities in Asia Minor occurred in the aftermath of the First World War during the struggle among the Turks, Greeks, Armenians, and European powers for what had been Ottoman territory. The young state of Turkey drew upon a bitter well of national sentiment in repelling all attempts on Asia Minor; it is one of the greatest tragedies of this century that this was accompanied by much violence and innocent suffering. The Greeks who escaped resettled in Greece, naming their communities — such as New Smyrna and New Philadelphia, both now prosperous sections of greater Athens — after the cities of their birth.

The Letters to the Seven Churches

Whether we accept the view of Edgar J. Goodspeed that St. John's letters to the Seven Churches are an imitation of St. Paul's letters to seven churches (with the letter to Philemon being addressed to the church in Laodicea and the letter to the Ephesians as an introductory or covering letter), or merely recognize in the Seven Letters another sevenfold division of material upon which the Book of Revelation is based, the Seven Letters clearly were not intended to be sent out independently to the churches to which they were addressed.* These Seven Letters never had a separate existence apart from one another and from the book of which they are an integral part. They are artificial letters, written for the precise purpose of encouraging persecuted Christians to remain loyal, if necessary unto death.

The letters clearly show that the author was well acquainted with the conditions in each of the churches he addressed. He knew the members of the several churches intimately. He was familiar with their local geography and history. He knew of the worship of Artemis in Ephesus, of the distinguished history of Sardis, and of the tepid waters of Hierapolis near Laodicea. St. John assumes that the church is, in a sense, the city, and that the local congregation does not live apart from the city and its inhabitants, believing, as Sir William M. Ramsay says, that "the church is all that is real in the city." The Seven Letters also show that their author felt a deep sense of responsibility for the congregations in Asia Minor, for he writes with unhesitating and unlimited authority. His tone of authority goes far beyond that of the Apostles. In fact, he presents Christ as the speaker in these Seven Letters, though the words are obviously those of St. John himself.

When these letters were written all the Seven Churches were in the Roman province of Asia and had been under Roman administration for more than two hundred years. The

---

* The main divisions of Revelation are: 1. The Seven Seal Vision, 6:1-8:6; 2. The Seven Trumpet Woes, 8:7-11:5; 3. The Seven Visions of the Dragon's Kingdom, 12:1-13:18; 4. The Seven Visions of Worshipers of the Lamb and of the Beast, 14:1-20; 5. The Seven Visions of the Bowls of God's Wrath, 15:1-16:21; 6. The Seven Visions of the Fall of "Babylon" or Rome, 17:1-19:10; 7. The Seven Visions of the End of Satan's Age and the Beginning of God's Righteous Age, 19:11-21:8.

Roman province of Asia included most of the western half of Asia Minor, with the regions of Caria, Lydia, Phrygia, Mysia and the coastlands of the Troad, Aeolis, and Ionia. The cities of the province of Asia had adopted Greek ways, and the Greek language had replaced the native tongues. Formally, the state religion was the worship of the Roman emperor or of Rome and the emperor. In practice, however, in several instances the cult of the emperor became associated with the local deity.

There were, of course, in addition to the Seven Churches mentioned by St. John, other Christian communities in Asia. Colossae had a church to which St. Paul addressed a letter in which he mentions a church in Hierapolis (Col 4:13). Troas also had a church (II Cor. 2:12, Acts 20:7 ff). There were churches in Magnesia and Tralles as there was in Cyzicus, situated on one of the great routes on which the Christian Gospel was carried.

The selection of the Seven Churches of the Revelation is significant in so far as they were on the great circular road connecting the most populous, wealthy, and influential cities of the province of Asia. Furthermore, it seems that the province was divided into seven dioceses corresponding to seven postal districts, each having as its center one of the seven cities. For the northern region with Troas, Adramyttium, and perhaps Cyzicus, the center was Pergamum. Thyatira served the inland district of the northeastern part of the province, while Sardis was the center for the middle Hermus Valley. Philadelphia was the "open door" (Rev. 3:8) for the district of Upper Lydia, and Laodicea was the center for the Lycus Valley and central Phrygia. Ephesus served the Cayster and Lower Meander Valleys and Smyrna the lower Hermus Valley and the North Ionian coasts.

Although spread throughout the province of Asia, all the Seven Churches are considered in Revelation to have the same two hostile forces threatening their congregational life. One is the secret and internal power of the Nicolaitan heresy, and the other is the imperial power demanding worship of the

29

emperor. Two of the Seven Churches are considered to have succumbed to these powers; Sardis is dead, and Laodicea is rejected. In contrast, two churches, Smyrna and Philadelphia, are unreservedly praised. Pergamum and Thyatira are treated with mingled praise and blame, while Ephesus will fall from its high position.

Although these Seven Churches are the particular concern of the author, nonetheless these Seven Letters are addressed to all churches, making them open letters to all Christians. Every generation has gained strength and comfort from them. As part of the Book of Revelation, however, they have been sadly exploited by extremists of every kind who have given their own prejudiced interpretations to all sections of the Apocalypse.

After a brief preface which includes the original title of the book, "the revelation of Jesus Christ," John introduces the letters to the Seven Churches with a covering letter (Rev. 1:4-20), in which he explains their purpose and gives an account of his vision of the celestial Christ, Who is represented as the actual author of the letters. Grace and peace is offered "from him who is and who was and who is to come," from the "seven spirits," and from "Jesus Christ the faithful witness." As had St. Paul and the other apostles, St. John expected the second coming of Christ to be soon, for he used the present tense "behold, he is coming with the clouds, and every eye will see him, every one who pierced him" (Rev. 1:7). When he writes "I John, your brother" (Rev. 1:9), he avoids any suggestion that he is either an apostle or one of the Twelve; on the contrary, he identifies himself with the brethren he addresses. His ecstatic experience of the divine commision is briefly described. "I was in the Spirit on the Lord's day, and I heard behind me a loud voice like a trumpet saying, 'Write what you see in a book and send it to the seven churches' " (Rev. 1:10-11). His vision is couched in the symbolic forms of the old apocalyptic vocabulary, obscuring his intention from outsiders and at the same time heightening his appeal to Christian readers.

I saw seven golden lampstands, and in the midst of the lampstands one like a son of man, clothed with a long robe and a golden girdle round his breast; his head and his hair were white as white wool, white as snow; his eyes were like a flame of fire, his feet were like burnished bronze, refined as in a furnace, and his voice was like the sound of many waters; in his right hand he held seven stars, from his mouth issued a sharp two-edged sword, and his face was like the sun shining in full strength.

When I saw him, I fell at his feet as though dead. But he laid his right hand upon me saying, "Fear not, I am the first and the last, and the living one; I died, and behold I am alive for evermore, and I have the keys of Death and Hades. Now write what you see, what is and what is to take place hereafter. As for the mystery of the seven stars which you saw in my right hand, and the seven golden lampstands, the seven stars are the angels of the seven churches and the seven lampstands are the seven churches.

Rev. 1:12b-20

Sample of Late Roman *uncial* Writing (Luke 12: 54-57)

To the Church in Ephesus

ON ANCIENT EPHESUS

Ephesus, the first of the Seven Churches addressed by St. John, remains the most impressive of all the sites we shall visit in the course of our reflections about the Seven Churches in Asia. The ruins of this city call forth a number of associations. Classicists and historians think of the ancient Ionian city or the capital of the Roman province of Asia. Bible students think of St. Paul's ministry and his literary activities, others connect Ephesus with St. John and the last days of the life of the Holy Virgin.

Ephesus had long been a religious center. Before the arrival of the Greeks, sacrifices were offered in Ephesus to the great mother-goddess Cybele, who later became identified with the Greek goddess Artemis. The archaic Temple of Artemis was built, entirely of marble, in the 6th century B.C., the golden age of the Ionian cities. Pliny the Elder (23-79 A.D.) explains that this temple was constructed on marshy soil to safeguard it against earthquakes. For centuries pilgrims from all over the ancient world assembled annually in Ephesus to offer their sacrifices to the goddess. Her temple, known as the Artemision, was one of the finest achievements of Hellenic art and architecture.

In the middle of the 6th century Ephesus was captured by Croesus, the king of Lydia, who added to the temple by sending columns and golden calves to beautify and extend the sanctuary. In 546 B.C. Ephesus became part of the Persian satrapy of Ionia. When Xerxes returned from his exploits in Greece in 478 B.C., he honored the Temple of Artemis, although he permitted other Ionian shrines to be sacked. After the defeat of the Persians at the Eurymedon River in

Ephesus: Theater and Hellenistic Agora

466 B.C., Ephesus became a tributary of Athens. Badly damaged during these upheavals, the Artemision was restored in 450 B.C. In the beginning of the 4th century B.C. the city fell again for a short time under Persian administration.

In 356 B.C., on the night, it was said, Alexander the Great was born, Herostratus, a madman in search of fame, set the temple on fire. The citizens erected another and more splendid temple with money collected by selling jewelry and other personal belongings in addition to the pillars of the former temple. When Alexander came to Ephesus in 334 B.C. the temple was still unfinished and the Macedonian emperor offered to finance the completion of the building if his generosity were credited on the architrave. The Ephesians, however, replied to Alexander that it was inappropriate for a god to dedicate offerings to gods. The Artemision had increased so much in fame that the 2nd century B.C. epigrammatist Antipater of Sidon included it in his list of the "Seven Wonders of the World," together with the Pyramids of Egypt, the Hanging Gardens of Semiramis in Babylon, the Statue of Zeus in Olympia, the Mausoleum at Halicarnassus, the Colossus at Rhodes, and the Pharos of Alexandria.

After Alexander's death, Ephesus was ruled by Lysimachus, who introduced fresh Greek colonists and renamed the city after his wife Arsinoë, but the old name prevailed. Among many building projects, Lysimachus enclosed the city with a wall almost six miles long. The westernmost tower of this wall is the traditional prison of St. Paul. When the city passed under Seleucid rule it continued to prosper, becoming the largest trading center in Asia Minor. After the defeat of Antiochus the Great, the Seleucid king, by the Romans, Ephesus was attached to the kingdom of Pergamum. In 133 B.C. Attalus III of Pergamum bequeathed the city with the rest of his possessions to the Romans, who made it the capital of the Roman province of Asia, the richest province in Asia Minor.

The Ephesians did not relish Roman rule. In the war

between Rome and Mithradates, King of Pontus, the Ephesians sided with Mithradates, killing those Romans who had fled to the Artemision, despite the right of asylum which the temple provided. In the Roman civil wars of the 1st century B.C., the Ephesians twice supported the unsuccessful party, offering help first to Brutus and Cassius, and then to Anthony.

Despite these troubles the city flourished, becoming the principal trading center of Roman Asia, and many splendid buildings, such as the theater, the odeum, the famous library of Celsus, the gymnasium, and numerous temples were built by the Romans. Pliny called Ephesus the "great luminary of Asia," and the 1st century B.C. geographer Strabo referred to the city as "the greatest emporium of Asia." The Artemision was still regarded as a place of refuge as in earlier times, though the limits of the refuge repeatedly had been changed. Strabo wrote that the limits of the refuge had been extended to include half the city. This proved harmful for it placed the city in the hands of criminals, and, therefore, this extension was nullified by Caesar Augustus.

APOSTOLIC EPHESUS

The beginnings of Christianity in Ephesus are shrouded in mystery. Perhaps we should accept the statement by the 2nd century bishop Irenaeus of Lyons that St. Paul founded the church in Ephesus; perhaps we should accept the tradition that St. John the beloved disciple settled with Mary, the mother of Our Lord, in Ephesus after the ascension of Christ. The apocryphal Travels and Miracles of St. John the Theologian refer to St. John's ministry in Ephesus before his banishment and record among other things the miracle of the raising of young Domnus in the city of Diana. However the Christian faith came to Ephesus, it was established there by the middle of the first century.

According to the Acts of the Apostles, St. Paul visited Ephesus on his return from the second missionary journey, which had taken him to Macedonia and Achaia. In the autumn of 51, accompanied by his fellow tentmakers Aquila and

Priscilla, he sailed from Cenchraea, the eastern harbor of Corinth, to Ephesus. Today Ephesus has no harbor and gives the impression of being an inland city, but in St. Paul's time Ephesus was an active port. After disembarking, St. ·Paul passed through the magnificent Harbor Gate at the western end of the road leading to the theater. This wide marble paved road eventually became known as the Arcadian Way in honor of the emperor Arcadius (383-408 A.D.), who enlarged and restored it.

During his brief stay in Ephesus, St. Paul visited the local synagogue, probably on the Sabbath day when the people were assembled, and "argued with the Jews" (Acts 18:19). Although the Jews had asked him to stay for a longer period, he declined, for the departure of his ship was imminent. The Western or Bezan text included in the King James version gives us the reason for the Apostle's decision to leave Ephesus, "I must by all means keep this feast that cometh in Jerusalem" (Acts 18:21). Although the existence of a synagogue in Ephesus is well attested, we have no indication of its location. Probably it was on the northern outskirts of the

St. John Raises Young Domnus from the Dead, in Ephesus
17th century wall painting from the Monastery of St. John (Exonarthex), Patmos

city near the harbor because of the need for water for ritual purposes. In addition to a menorah carved into the steps leading to the 2nd century A.D. Library of Celsus, the only archaeological remains indicating a Jewish colony in Ephesus during the Hellenistic and Roman periods are several terracotta lamps with the menorah, and a unique glass with the menorah and the *shofar* on the left and the *lulab* on the right. Both the lamps and the glass were found in the cemetery of the Seven Sleepers.

There were major Jewish communities in many cities of Asia, such as Smyrna (Rev. 2:9), Pergamum (Rev. 2:14), Thyatira (Rev. 2:20), Philadelphia (Rev. 3:9), but also in places like Laodicea, Apamea, Miletus, and others. The Seleucid ruler Antiochus II Theos (261-247 B.C.) granted full citizenship to these Jews, who had migrated from Babylon to the Ionian cities. In Ephesus they enjoyed many privileges. They were Roman citizens, but were exempt from military service and were permitted to live according to their laws. The 1st century A.D. Jewish historian Flavius Josephus records a Roman decree stating:

> Whereas the Jews in the city have petitioned the proconsul Marcus Junius Brutus, son of Pontius, that they might observe their Sabbaths and do all those things which are in accordance with their native customs without interference from anyone, and the governor has granted their request, it has therefore been decreed by the council and the people that as the matter is of concern to the Romans, no one shall be prevented from keeping the Sabbath days nor be fined from doing so.

We may reasonably assume that similar privileges were issued to the Jews of the other cities addressed by St. John.

While St. Paul sailed on to Caesarea, Aquila and Priscilla remained in Ephesus where they became pillars of the local congregation. Ephesian Christianity may well consider them the organizers of the first church in the province of Asia.

Aquila, a Jew from the Roman province of Pontus on the shores of the Euxine (Black Sea), and Priscilla, his Roman wife, had been expelled from Rome under an edict issued by the emperor Claudius in 49 A.D. They went to Corinth where they met St. Paul, who "went to see them, and because he was of the same trade he stayed with them, and they worked, for by trade they were tentmakers" (Acts 18:2, 3). There is no indication that Aquila and Priscilla were Christians before they met St. Paul, and it is probable that their friendship with the Apostle resulted in their conversion. Once in Ephesus, they assisted in laying the foundations for St. Paul's future ministry in this city.

One day, Apollos, an Alexandrian Jew and eloquent orator, arrived in Ephesus. "He had been instructed in the way of the Lord; and being fervent in spirit, he spoke and taught accurately the things concerning Jesus, though he knew only the baptism of John. He began to speak boldly in the synagogue; but when Priscilla and Aquila heard him, they took him and expounded to him the way of God more accurately" (Acts 18:25,26). Apollos had succeeded in attracting several Jews who accepted his teaching, for when St. Paul returned to Ephesus in the fall of 54, he encountered a sectarian fellowship of followers of John the Baptist, of whom Apollos was probably the principal spokesman. St. Luke called them "disciples" (Acts 19:1), though they had neither heard of the Holy Spirit nor had they been baptized in the name of Jesus. "On hearing this, they were baptized in the name of the Lord Jesus. And when Paul had laid his hands upon them, the Holy Spirit came on them; and they spoke with tongues and prophesied. There were about twelve of them in all" (Acts 19:5-7).

Three years after his first visit, St. Paul returned to the Ephesian synagogue where he proclaimed the message of the Kingdom of God. While in some places the whole Jewish community had rejected the Apostle, in Ephesus only "some were stubborn and disbelieved," though they included the leaders of the synagogue. After three months of preaching in the synagogue, St. Paul was evicted, though fortunately he was able to use the hall of Tyrannus, probably himself a rhetorician, which was rented to visiting lecturers. To the many strangers in Ephesus St. Paul would have appeared as one of those numerous traveling philosophers or sophists who moved from town to town to share their wisdom. The Western text adds that the Apostle taught "from the fifth to the tenth hour," i.e. from 11 A.M. to 4 P.M., during the heat of the day, a schedule he may have kept for almost two years.

Through St. Paul's preaching, Christian congregations were established throughout the Roman province of Asia, and among them were the remaining six of the Seven Churches. We do not know whether St. Paul traveled to the various cities or whether people from them came to Ephesus to listen to the Apostle and subsequently organized congregations. The reference "that all the residents of Asia heard the word of the Lord, both Jews and Greeks" (Acts 19:10) implies that, by the latter part of the first century when the Acts of the Apostles were compiled by St. Luke, Christian congregations were well established in the province of Asia.

During his stay in Ephesus St. Paul continued to minister to the churches he had established in Achaia, Macedonia, and Asia Minor. One day, while at work, visitors from Corinth brought him disturbing news. The First and Second Letter to the Corinthians, written from Ephesus, are his counsel to this problem infested congregation. In addition, St. Paul interrupted his stay in Ephesus at least once to visit his Corinthian converts.

Ephesus, with its temple of Artemis, "she whom all Asia and the world worship" (Acts 19:27), attracted people from all over Asia Minor for religious and business purposes. Among the numerous visitors from the province of Galatia were Christians who informed the Apostle that Jewish Christians had spread a legalistic type of Christianity among the Galatian churches of Pisidian Antioch, Iconium, Lystra, and Derbe, churches which St. Paul had organized during his first missionary journey (Acts 13:14 - 14:23). These Jewish Christians, or Judaizers, maintained that one had to be or become a descendant of Abraham to benefit from the

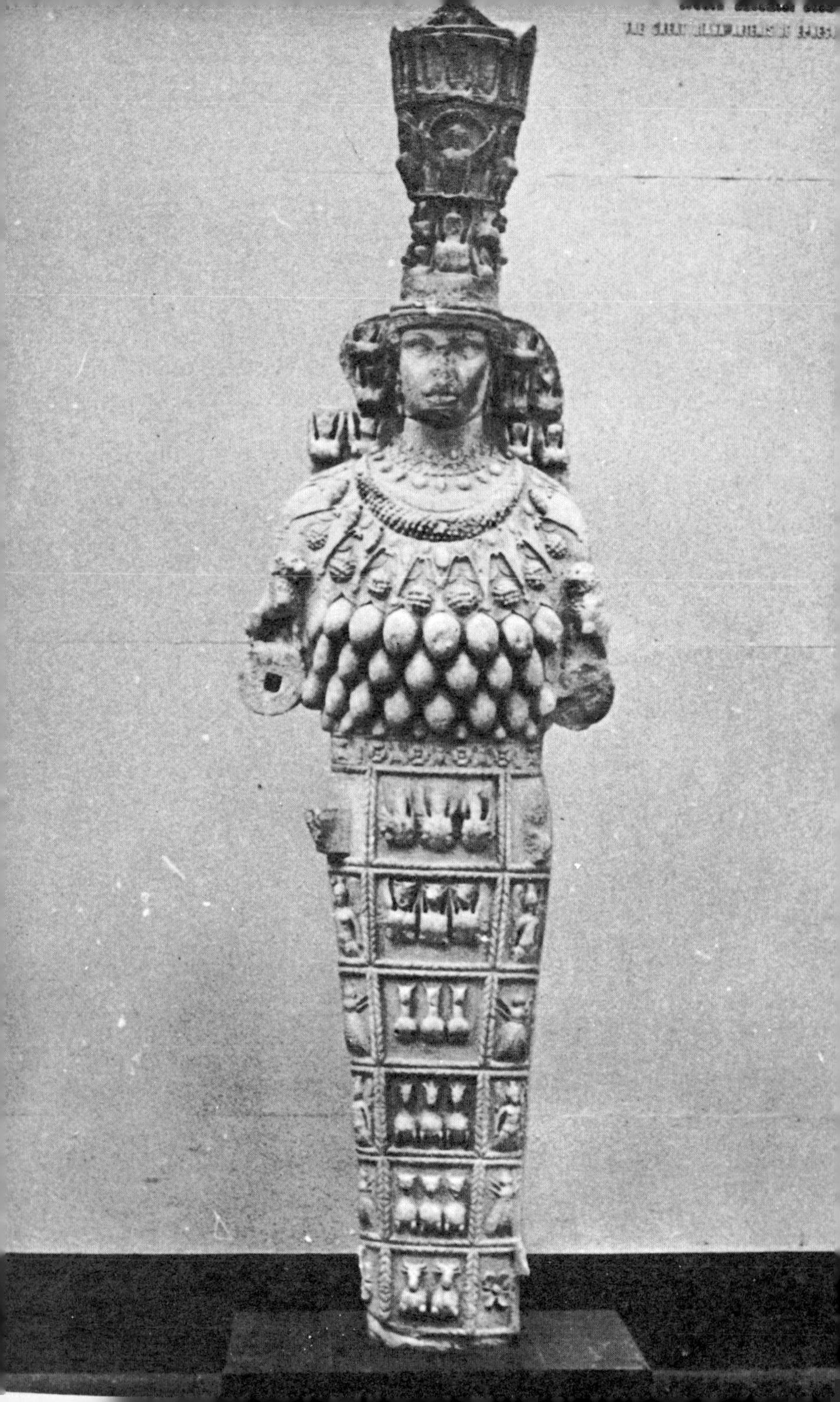

blessings of Jesus Christ. The only way to enter the church, therefore, was through the synagogue. Unable to leave Ephesus, St. Paul dictated a circular letter "to the churches in Galatia" (Gal. 1:2), in which he contrasts the power of faith unto salvation with the adherence to the law.

Although St. Luke does not mention that the Apostle Paul was imprisoned in Ephesus, Paul himself, in his correspondence with the churches in Corinth, Philippi, and Colossae, repeatedly referred to his sufferings. To the church in Corinth he wrote, "for we do not want you to be ignorant, brethren, of the affliction we experienced in Asia; for we were so utterly, unbearably crushed that we despaired of life itself. Why, we felt that we had received the sentence of death" (II Cor. 1:8, 9). On another occasion he spoke of his fight with beasts at Ephesus (I Cor. 15:32). The apocryphal Acts of Paul has elaborated on the Apostle's imprisonment. While in prison, Eubola and Artemilla, wives of eminent Ephesians and loyal disciples of St. Paul, visited him by night requesting to be baptized by him. Miraculously, St. Paul's iron fetters were loosed and, unrecognized, he left the prison with his disciples and baptized them by the seashore. He returned to prison without any of the guards realizing he had been gone. In another apocryphal story "a lion of huge size and unmatched strength was let loose upon St. Paul, and it ran to him in the stadium and lay down at his feet." Neither the lion nor any of the other savage beasts, however, touched him. Finally, a vast and violent hailstorm poured down and "shattered the heads" of many men and saved the Apostle's life.

Local Ephesian tradition has identified the large square tower near the port as the prison of St. Paul. The building is on the western end of Mount Coressos and was an integral part of the wall built by Lysimachus. Western travelers from the 17th century onwards are consistent in their reports that they were shown this structure as the Apostle's prison.

First Century Statue of Diana of Ephesus
Ephesus Museum, Selçuk

St. Paul was permitted to receive numerous visitors during his imprisonment. As is evident from his letters from prison, Epaphroditus, from the church in Philippi, delivered the gifts from the Macedonian Christians to the imprisoned Apostle, to which Paul replied in the Letter to the Philippians. About the same time Onesimus, a young runaway slave probably from Laodicea, appeared at the prison gate in Ephesus. He had robbed his master Philemon, and somehow he expected St. Paul to free him from slavery. The Apostle would have liked to keep Onesimus "in order that he might serve me on your behalf during my imprisonment for the gospel" (Philem. 13), though for Onesimus's own sake it was necessary to send him back to the master he had wronged. Instead of just sending him back, however, St. Paul gave him a letter addressed to Philemon commending Onesimus as a trustworthy Christian and appealing to Philemon to forgive the young slave and receive him as a beloved brother. Philemon not only received Onesimus back, but may even have freed him. About sixty years later, Ignatius of Antioch wrote a letter from Smyrna to the church in Ephesus in which he spoke very highly of their bishop Onesimus. We cannot be certain that Onesimus, the third bishop of Ephesus (ca. 107-117), was the runaway slave Onesimus, but he may well have been.

Probably soon after the arrival of Onesimus in Ephesus, Epaphras, the leader of the church in Colossae, came to St. Paul troubled about the dissatisfaction of the Colossian Christians. The Colossian church was threatened by several syncretic heresies and divided by theological speculation. In his Letter to the Colossians, the Apostle stressed the adequacy of Jesus Christ. He sent the letter with Tychicus (Col. 4:7), who accompanied Onesimus on his return to Philemon.

In the meantime, St. Paul's situation was deteriorating. Several Christians visiting him in Ephesus were arrested by the Roman authorities. Thus we hear of Aristarchus of Thessalonica; Mark, the cousin of Barnabas; Jesus Justus;

Epaphras of Colossae; Luke, the beloved physician; and a man named Demas sharing his imprisonment (Col 4:10).

While imprisoned, St. Paul composed the last and most comprehensive letter he sent to the churches in Asia. Generally known as the Letter to the Ephesians, this document was probably an encyclical letter addressed to many churches, for the words "in Ephesus" are omitted in two of the best and earliest Greek manuscripts, the Codex Sinaiticus and the Codex Vaticanus. The Letter to the Ephesians is the most general of St. Paul's letters and stresses the unity and divinity of the entire church. Tychicus, "the beloved brother and faithful minister in the Lord" (Eph. 6:21), who carried the letter, read it to the several congregations, inserting each time the appropriate name of the church.

We do not know when St. Paul was released, although we do know that he immediately returned to work among the Jews and the Gentiles. St. Luke describes St. Paul's successful dealings with the Ephesian exorcists (Acts 19:11 - 20). Of all the cities in Asia, Ephesus was best known for the study of magic and the occult arts. Is it surprising, therefore, that some of the itinerant Jewish exorcists applied the proven name of the Lord Jesus to effect healings and exorcisms? The result, as St. Luke records it, was devastating, for the evil spirits overpowered the exorcists and beat them. This extraordinary event led some Ephesians to be converted to the Christian faith and to destroy their books on magic. The overpowering of the Ephesian exorcists and the conversions which followed were such significant successes in the Apostle's career that he felt able to leave the city of Artemis for Macedonia and Achaia.

Before he left, however, St. Paul became involved in the famous silversmiths' riot (Acts 19:23 - 20:1), which took place in the Ephesian theater at the intersection of Marble Street and the Arcadian Way. The motive for the riot was primarily economic, in so far as St. Paul's preaching must have threatened the business of the silversmiths who made silver votive offerings for the Temple of Artemis. After the silversmith Demetrius gathered the members of his guild and told them that St. Paul taught that the images were worthless, the silversmiths moved to the theater where they and others who joined them shouted for two hours, "Great is Artemis of the Ephesians." Finally, the town clerk entered the theater and quieted the people, convincing them that the supremacy of Artemis was not in peril, that the Christians had neither robbed the temple nor blasphemed the goddess, and that for any complaints the courts or the proconsuls were available. Once the uproar had ceased, St. Paul sent for his disciples and, having spoken with them, left for Macedonia and Achaia.

While in Corinth, St. Paul remembered his friends in Ephesus. The last chapter of St. Paul's Letter to the Romans (Rom. 16:1 - 24) is generally accepted as having been written to the Christians in Ephesus. Phoebe, a deaconess of the church in Cenchreae, the eastern harbor of Corinth, was about to sail for the city of Artemis, and the Apostle used this opportunity to send greetings to his numerous friends in Ephesus. There were "Prisca and Aquila," who had "risked their necks" for the Apostle, and who were hosts to one of the Ephesian house churches (Rom. 16:3 - 5). A special greeting was extended to the "beloved Epaenetus, who was the first convert in Asia for Christ" (Rom. 16:5), and to Andronicus and Junius who had been his fellow prisoners and who were "men of note among the apostles" (Rom. 16:7). There was also Stachys, his beloved friend (Rom. 16:9), who may have been the leader of the house church in Hierapolis, where Philip proclaimed the Gospel. In conclusion, the Apostle warned his Ephesian brethren against those "who create dissensions and difficulties." To his final greetings are joined those of Timothy, Lucius of Cyrene (Acts 13:1), Jason of Thessalonica (Acts 17:5 - 9), Sosipater of Veria (Acts 20:4), Gaius, Quartus, Erastus the city treasurer, and Tertius the scribe who wrote the letter.

St. Paul did not return to Ephesus. At the end of his third missionary journey, in the spring of 57, St. Paul stopped briefly in Miletus "for he had decided to sail past Ephesus, so that he might not have to spend time in Asia" (Acts 20:16). In Miletus the Apostle delivered to the elders of the Ephesian church one of the most touching sermons recorded in the Acts of the Apostles (Acts 20:18 - 36). He was deeply concerned about the threats to the internal unity of the Ephesian church, and he admonished them to remain alert. The final experience of the Ephesian elders with the Apostle was one of prayer and deep sorrow that they should see his face no more (Acts 20:38).

The impact of St. Paul's ministry in Ephesus was to last for a long time. Towards the end of the 1st century, Ephesian disciples of St. Paul assembled the various letters written by the Apostle and joined them into what may be called the Pauline corpus addressed to seven churches; Rome, Corinth, Galatia, Philippi, Colossae, Thessalonica, and Laodicea (Philemon), with the so-called Letter to the Ephesians as a covering letter. This collection may well have inspired St. John to begin his Revelation with letters to the Seven Churches of Asia. As Edgar J. Goodspeed points out: "His (St. John's) book is so swayed by the newly published corpus of Paul's letters to seven churches that he actually begins his book with a corpus of letters to seven churches. If any literary resemblance could be more striking and massive than this, it is difficult to imagine what it would be." The collector of the Pauline corpus has remained anonymous, though he may have been Onesimus of Ephesus, who was familiar with St. Paul's letters to the Colossians and to Philemon. A few years later other collections of letters were assembled in Asia as, for example, St. Ignatius's seven letters as well as the three letters written by St. John the Elder.

St. Paul left Timothy behind in Ephesus to "charge certain persons not to teach any different doctrine" (I Tim. 1:3). Eusebius, the 4th century church historian, wrote that "Timothy is recorded as having first received the episcopate at Ephesus" and, during the reign of Domitian while John was exiled to Patmos, Timothy is said to have suffered martyrdom by being clubbed to death by the mob for protesting against the orgies associated with the cult of Artemis. In the 6th century there was a martyrium of Timothy on Mount Pion in Ephesus.

Although Ephesus was the cult center of the goddess Artemis, the imperial worship was not neglected. Early in the reign of Augustus, a large altar to the emperor was placed in the sacred precinct of the Artemision. Later, additional temples of the imperial cult were built. Many cities were eager to build a temple for imperial worship, but this could be done only with imperial permission. The privilege carried with it the title of "Neocorus" or Temple Warden, which was granted to Ephesus four times by different emperors.

As the Christians in other centers of Asia Minor, so the Christians in Ephesus were harrassed by the Roman authorities.

"To the angel of the church in Ephesus write: 'The words of him who holds the seven stars in his right hand, who walks among the seven golden lampstands.

" 'I know your works, your toil and your patient endurance, and how you cannot bear evil men but have tested those who call themselves apostles but are not, and found them to be false; I know you are enduring patiently and bearing up for my name's sake, and you have not grown weary. But I have this against you, that you have abandoned the love you had at first. Remember then from what you have fallen, repent and do the works you did at first. If not, I will come to you and remove your lampstand from its place, unless you repent. Yet this you have, you hate the works of the Nicolaitans, which I also hate. He who has an ear, let him hear what the Spirit says to the churches. To him who conquers I will grant to eat of the tree of life, which is in the paradise of God.'

Rev. 2:1 - 7

St. John's letter to the Ephesians, as does his letter to the church in Sardis, mixes praise and blame. The Ephesians are praised for their work, toil, patient endurance, and refusal to be led astray by false teachers. All is not perfect, for there has been a decline in their original love; the enthusiasm of the young church had cooled with age. This censure, however, is offset by praise for their hatred of the works of the Nicolaitans, the false apostles. The reference "to him who conquers" is to the Christian who endures his persecution. He will be given to eat from the tree of life "with its twelve kinds of fruit, yielding its fruit each month" (Rev. 22:2). While the letter is laudatory, it lacks the cordiality and sympathy of the letters to the Smyrnaeans and Philadelphians.

According to Eusebius, John returned from Patmos to Ephesus, from which he traveled to the neighboring regions of the Gentiles appointing bishops and instituting new churches. St. John died in Ephesus during the reign of Trajan (98-117).

HISTORICAL NOTES ON THE CHURCH IN EPHESUS

In approximately the year 105, St. Ignatius of Antioch, on his way to Rome, was met in Ephesus by Onesimus, Bishop of Ephesus, whom Ignatius described as "a man of inexpressable love." Later, St. Ignatius praised the Ephesians, saying: "you all live according to truth and no heresy dwells among you . . . I have learnt, however, that some from elsewhere have stayed with you, who have evil doctrine, but you did not suffer them to sow it among you." By the latter part of the 2nd century Ephesus was an important enough Christian center for Polycrates of Ephesus to rank as the senior bishop of the dioceses of Asia.

In 431 the Third Ecumenical Council convened in Ephesus to settle the christological dispute between Nestorius, archbishop of Constantinople, and Cyril, archbishop of Alexandria, both of whom claimed primacy of the East. In November 430 Cyril convened the bishops of the East in Alexandria to examine the christological doctrines of Nestorius. The doctrines were found heretical, and Cyril issued the *Twelve Anathemata*. If Nestorius did not endorse these doctrinal statements, he was to be deposed. Nestorius rejected them, and the need for an ecumenical council became acute. In the spring of 431 the emperor Theodosius II convoked a council in the Church of the Holy Virgin in Ephesus, the ruins of which can still be visited. On the opening day 159 bishops attended the council, though the number increased as the sessions went on. Nestorius, who refused to appear, was deposed from his see and excommunicated for his heretical teachings.

According to tradition, seven young princes of the imperial court embraced the Christian faith in Ephesus and took the names Maximianus, Malchus, Martianus, Constantinus, Dionysius, John, and Serapion. During the persecutions of the emperor Decius (249 - 251), they were ordered to publicly offer sacrifices to idols. They refused and fled to a cave at the foot of a nearby mountain. Their malefactors closed up the cave and the seven young princes slept for almost 200 years. In 446, during the reign of Theodosius II, the young princes rose from their sleep. The wall entombing them had crumbled, and they sent Malchus to the nearest village to buy food. The shopkeeper discovered the miracle when the youth offered to pay with an old imperial coin. The news of the "resurrection" of the Seven Sleepers spread rapidly to the imperial court, and the emperor traveled to Ephesus to verify the story, but before he arrived the young princes died. In commemoration of this miracle, Theodosius II built a basilica enshrining the youths' cave.

From the middle of the 5th century onwards, Ephesus ranked as second metropolis of the patriarchate of Constantinople, and by the beginning of the 6th century the metropolitan of Ephesus ruled over 36 suffragan sees. Some of the better known bishops of Ephesus were the 5th century Memnon, Basil, and Bassianus, who built a hospital for the poor with 70 beds in Ephesus. Bassianus, we are told, was consecrated Bishop of Ephesus by 40 bishops instead of by the patriarch. During the 5th and 6th centuries the Ephesian church professed Monophysitism — belief in the One Nature of Christ — championed by Alexandria, rather than

Dyophysitism, — belief in both the human and divine natures of Christ — championed by Rome and Constantinople.

In the 6th century Justinian built a splendid basilica over the tomb of St. John. Procopius of Caesarea, the 6th century Byzantine historian, wrote that the emperor "tore down to the ground a small church in ruined condition and replaced it by a church so large and beautiful, that so to speak briefly, it resembles very closely in all respects, and is a rival to, the shrine which he dedicated to all the Apostles in the imperial city."

Despite such growth, the city's history was stormy. In 655 and again in 717 Ephesus was briefly occupied by the Arabs. During the 8th and 9th century the iconoclastic controversy brought persecution to both the iconodules, who venerated icons, and the iconoclasts, who considered such veneration idolatry. Two Ephesian bishops, Hypatius and Theophilus, were martyred by the iconoclasts. Throughout the controversy most monks remained iconodules, and in 663 general Lachanodracon had 38 monks of the Monastery of Pelecete in Bithynia put to death in the public square of Ephesus.

After being forced to abdicate in 1078, Michael VII Ducas exchanged the imperial scepter for the episcopal staff and became bishop of Ephesus for a short time. In 1090 the city was captured and pillaged by the Selçuk Turks, and it never regained its former prominence.

Alexius I Comnenus (1081 - 1118) succeeded in retaking the city, renaming it Haghios Theologos, after St. John the Theologian, but the Turks repeatedly raided the city in the 12th century. Odo of Deuil reported in the mid-12th century that the tomb of St. John was surrounded by walls to keep the pagans out, and that there were ruins in Ephesus. The 12th century Arab geographer Idrisi described Ephesus as a city in ruins, and another 12th century visitor reported that the Church of St. John was in such a dilapidated state that tesserae from the mosaic decoration fell upon the head of the metropolitan during the celebration of the liturgy.

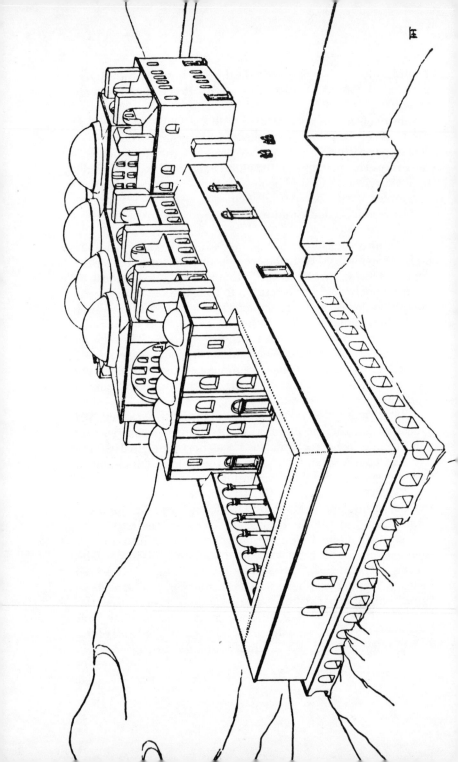

Throughout its Byzantine life, however, Ephesus remained a favorite Christian pilgrimage site. In 1106 - 07 the Russian abbot Daniel visited the tomb of St. John and reported that, on the anniversary of St. John's death, a holy dust arose from the tomb and was collected by believers as a cure for diseases. He visited the remains of the 300 Holy Fathers and St. Alexander, the cave of the Seven Sleepers, the tomb of Mary Magdalene, and the coffin of the Apostle Timothy. He also saw the image of the Holy Virgin which had been used to refute Nestorius. Two hundred years later Ramon Muntaner - Buchon witnessed miracles at the tomb of St. John and wrote that the exudations of the tomb were beneficial for childbirth, fever, and would calm a stormy sea.

At the beginning of the 13th century the metropolitan of Ephesus, Nicholas Mesarites, played a major role in the theological discussions between the Byzantines and the Latins. In 1304 Ephesus was occupied and plundered by the Turks, but they were driven out by the Catalans in the service of the Byzantines two years later. Apparently the city remained without a resident metropolitan for many years for, although Matthew, Metropolitan of Ephesus, is first mentioned in a synodical document of 1329, he remained in Constantinople for ten years. Ephesus may have been without a resident metropolitan from the time the city was taken by the Turks in 1304 until Matthew's arrival in 1339. Matthew had been able to proceed from Smyrna only after bribing Umur Beg, the ruler of Smyrna, for safe passage to Ephesus. Matthew's request that the cathedral, which had been turned into a mosque, be returned to him, however, was denied. The metropolitan had six priests and his parishioners numbered several thousands. Most of them were prisoners and slaves, although there also were many priests and monks.

In 1368 the Holy Synod, trying to strengthen the see of Ephesus, added to it the see of Pyrgion. Still, a year later even

Reconstruction of 6th Century Basilica of St. John in Ephesus (Selçuk)

Source: *Forschungen in Ephesos*, Vol. IV, 3, Wien, 1951

this territory could not support one priest so Ephesus received the metropolitan sees of Pergamum, New Phocaea, and Clazomenae. The city was retaken by the Turks in 1375, and badly damaged in 1402 when the Turks were defeated by Tamerlane. During the next several years the city was left pretty much on its own while Bayazid's sons fought for succesion, but the eventual winner, Murat II, occupied it in 1426. The city had so decayed that when Mark of Ephesus attended the Council of Florence in 1439, he was the shepherd of only a small miserable village. A metropolitan was still appointed in the 15th century, but there are no records about church life in Ephesus after the end of the 14th century. From 1318 to 1411 Ephesus had a series of Latin bishops in addition to the Orthodox clergy, for the Italians, who called the town Altoluogo, had established a commercial colony in the city.

For travelers to Ephesus in the 17th - 19th centuries, the city was a disappointment. In their reports they refer to the "Prison of St. Paul," a large square tower on the western end of Mount Coressos, which was part of the defensive wall built in the 3rd century B.C. by Lysimachus. They were shown a beautiful reddish-brown marble baptismal font of St. John. J. Aegidius van Egmont (1759) added that "here the Greeks and the Roman Catholics in our company endeavoured to break off small pieces to present to their friends as relics. It has all the marks of those vessels used here for pressing oil, being very shallow and raised in the middle." The Church of St. John, converted into a mosque, had two domes. In one dome the travelers were shown an arrow said to have been shot by Tamerlane. When James Emerson (1829) climbed the hill once surmounted by the Church of St. John, one of the most formidable buildings in the Byzantine Empire, he found "a heap of rubbish and grass-grown walls. Some large columns of granite are still left standing." Most of the travelers visited the ruins of the Church of the Seven Sleepers.

The travelers give a consistently depressing report about the Christian residents. Thomas Smith (1671) referred to the city as being "reduced to an inconsiderable number of cottages, wholly inhabited by Turks," and Richard Pococke (1739) reported that "there was not a single Christian within two leagues round Ephesus." On the other hand, Edmund Chishull (1698) reported from the nearby village of Kirkindje, today Serindje, which in his day was entirely Christian, that "the priest showed us a venerable manuscript written by Prochorus." Kirkindje, which van Egmont called "the melancholy remains of the ancient church of Ephesus," existed as a Christian village with the lineal descendants of the Ephesian Christians until 1922, when the Christians left as part of the great population exchange between Greece and Turkey.

In the 18th century the metropolitan of Ephesus resided in nearby Scala Nuova or Kushadasi, and in the beginning of the 19th century he moved to Vourla (Urla) on the nearby Gulf of Clazomenes. A few years later he moved to Magnesia-on-the-Meander. In the middle of the 19th century the metropolitan see included 58 towns and villages with 10,950 believers. None, however, remained after the 1922 population exchange.

CHRISTIAN RUINS IN EPHESUS

The Church of the Holy Virgin

The Church of the Holy Virgin is in the northwestern part of the city on the site of a 2nd century Roman building which has been identified either with the *museion* or the corn and money exchange. During the 4th century, probably around 350, the building was converted into a church, making it probably the first basilica, and certainly the first cathedral, dedicated to the Holy Virgin. It is 260 m. long and 30 m. wide, with three aisles, the central one finishing in a semicircular apse. It was supported by tall columns and adorned with beautiful mosaics. On the western end was a large square atrium and narthex with a mosaic floor. An octagonally shaped baptistry with a large and deep water basin of white marble is on the north side of the atrium; it is one of the best preserved baptistries of the Early Christian period. The

eastern section of the building served as the episcopal residence and offices. In 1930 a plaque was discovered in the narthex of the basilica on which the archbishop Hypatius (531 - 536) clearly indicated that this church was the site of the famous 3rd Ecumenical Council convened in Ephesus in 431. On July 26, 1967, Pope Paul VI offered supplications in the ruins of this historic sanctuary.

The Church of St. John

The Church of St. John is on a hilltop northwest of the ruins of Ephesus. It is on the edge of modern Selçuk, formerly known as Aya Soluk. According to an early tradition, St. John lived and was buried on this hill. The tomb was marked by a memorial until the 4th century when it was enclosed by a church, the so-called Theodosian basilica. In the 6th century Justinian demolished the basilica and built in its stead "the greatest and most magnificent church of early Christendom." This building was 120 m. long and 40 m. wide, with six large domes covering the center aisle and five small domes covering the narthex. The crypt of St. John containing his tomb was discovered beneath the holy of holies during the excavations in 1926. The central apse has an elaborate synthronos. In some places marble slabs and traces of floor mosaics can still be seen. The column capitals are adorned with monograms of the emperor Justinian and his wife Theodora. In the apse of the chapel (Kuçuk Kilise) north of the basilica are the remains of 10th century wall paintings, including one of St. John. Northwest of the nave of the basilica is the baptistry. The outside walls and superstructure of the basilica were built of brick.

In the beginning of the 14th century when Ephesus was occupied by the Turks, most of the valuable vessels of this church were pillaged. The basilica was probably destroyed in 1402 by Tamerlane, since graffiti of 1341 and 1387 inscribed by pilgrims still testify to its existence.

Ephesus: The Church of the Holy Virgin Mary

The Necropolis of the Seven Sleepers

The extensive Grotto of the Seven Sleepers of Ephesus, one of the most popular sites of medieval Christian pilgrimage, is at the foot of Mt. Pion. The emperor Theodosius II (408 - 450) built the church to enshrine the cave in which the seven young princes slept for almost 200 years. The 1927 - 1928 excavations by the Austrian Archaeological Institute have brought to light several buildings in the ravine. They include the church, built by Theodosius II above the catacomb system with 10 chambers; an extensive necropolis west and a mausoleum north of the Theodosian church; a large crypt with 400 tombs; a terrace-chapel; and the so-called unfinished Abradas mausoleum. More than 2,000 votive lamps were found during the excavations. The large number of 14th and 15th century graffiti by Frankish, Greek, and Armenian pilgrims adorning the walls of the church indicate the continuing popularity of the site as a place of pilgrimage. By the 17th century, however, the site is described as being in ruins.

The House of the Virgin

The House of the Holy Virgin, known by the Greek-Turkish hybrid name of Panaya Kapulu or the House of the All Holy, is on the summit of Bulbul Dagh. The tradition of the sojourn and dormition of the Holy Virgin in Ephesus is based upon the belief that St. John took St. Mary with him when he left Jerusalem for Asia after the ascension of Jesus Christ. According to the Gospel of St. John, the Apostle took her to his own home (John 19:27), a phrase some scholars interpret as "his home in Ephesus."

A 4th century tradition maintained that St. Mary lived in Ephesus, and by the early Middle Ages it was believed that "the Apostle John passed a great part of his life in Ephesus, and died there: as did the Virgin Mary and Mary Magdalene."

Selçuk: The Basilica of St. John

Until the latter part of the 19th century, Orthodox Christians of Kirkindje, descendants of Ephesian Christians, assembled annually on the Feast of the Assumption at Panaya Kapulu where the Divine Liturgy was celebrated. Thus the Kirkindje Christians retained for several centuries an early medieval tradition which would have vanished with their departure from Asia Minor in 1922 had it not been for the visions of the German Augustinian nun Catherine Emmerich (1774-1824), which revived interest in St. Mary's sojourn in Ephesus. In her visions, Sister Catherine accurately described the topography of the house in which, after Our Lord's ascension, St. Mary lived with St. John. "Her dwelling was on a hill to the left of the road from Jerusalem some three and a half hours from Ephesus . . . It was on this plateau that the Jewish settlers had made their home . . . John had a house built for the Holy Virgin before he brought her here . . . Mary's house was the only one built of stone." In 1891 Father Eugene Poulin, superior of the Lazarist College in Smyrna, followed Sister Catherine's description of the House of Mary and found the ruins of an ancient house which had been transformed into a chapel. Archaeologists have attributed different dates to the ruins, but some sections of the walls may date from the 1st century A.D. The tradition of the sojourn of the Holy Virgin in Ephesus is one of those beautiful gems of Christian piety and devotion which has led many pilgrims to a deeper appreciation of their Christian faith. Where people from all over the world once offered their devotion to Artemis-Diana, now devout Christians come to venerate the Holy Virgin Mary.

Ephesus: The House of the Holy Virgin Mary, Panaya Kapulu

To the Church in Smyrna

ON ANCIENT SMYRNA

The founding of Smyrna is shrouded in mythology. According to an early Byzantine tradition the site was first known as Tantalis, suggesting it had been founded by Tantalus, the mythological king of Sipylus in Lydia. Herodotus writes that Theseus named the city Smyrna after his Amazon wife, while others believed that the name derived from another Amazon called Smyrna. Others have related the name Smyrna to the precious spice used as a scent by brides and for general household and burial purposes. This domestic perfume was compounded from the germ resin of a small thorny tree, *balsamodendron Myrrha,* and known by the ancient Greeks as *smyrna.* The connection, if any, between the name of the city and the spice is still an unsolved mystery. In any case the name is of Anatolian origin.

Excavations by the University of Ankara unearthed traces of a small (second millenium B.C.) settlement at a place known as Tepekule near Bayrakli at the end of the gulf. In the 11th century B.C. Aeolian settlers from Lesbos and Cyme seized the region and founded a prosperous commercial center. Eventually, however, Smyrna passed into the hands of the Ionians of Colophon and became the 13th of the Ionian states. In the 7th century B.C. Smyrna shared in the general prosperity of Ionia and the city expanded, but soon it became the target of the Lydian kings. Though Gyges of Lydia (685-657 B.C.) was repulsed by the Smyrnaeans, Alyattes III (609-560 B.C.) sacked the city. In 546 B.C. Cyrus the Great of Persia conquered and defeated Croesus, the last king of Lydia, and Smyrna fell under Persian domination for two centuries.

Izmir: 2nd Century Agora

The city was refounded by Alexander the Great, who visited Smyrna after Sardis in 334 B.C. Pausanias states that as Alexander rested under a plane tree beside the sanctuary of the two Nemeseis on Mount Pagus, the goddesses appeared to him in his sleep and bade him found a city on that spot. After confirmation from the oracle of Apollo at Claros, the Smyrnaeans settled on the hill. The scheme was, according to Strabo, carried out by Antigonus (316-301 B.C.). Lysimachus (360-281 B.C.) enlarged and fortified the city.

The Smyrnaeans were among the first to recognize in Rome the future mistress of Asia. In 195 B.C., when the Seleucid kingdom was still at the height of its power, the Smyrnaeans built a temple to and instituted the worship of deified Rome. A century later, when a Smyrnaean public assembly learned of the distress in the Roman army during their war against Mithradates VI Eupator, the citizens stripped off their own clothes to send them to the shivering Romans. Smyrna shared with the other cities the miseries of the province of Asia under the Roman republic and enjoyed its prosperity under the empire. Cicero expressed the Roman sentiments about Smyrna when he called the city "our most faithful and most ancient ally." Strabo mentioned the library and the Homereium, a rectangular stoa containing a shrine and a wooden statue of Homer, "for the Smyrnaeans also lay special claim to the poet," believing he was born in their city. This belief was also held by the citizens of Rhodes, Colophon, Salamis, Chios, Argos, and Athens. The goddess of Smyrna was a local variety of Cybele, known as the Sipylene Mother.

Smyrna claimed to be "first in Asia," but so did Pergamum and Ephesus, and in one way or another all three cities deserved the title. Smyrna, nonetheless, claimed to be the largest of the Asian cities and the first in beauty. According to Philostratus the Athenian (170-245 A.D.), none of the cities of Europe were worthy to be compared with it.

APOSTOLIC SMYRNA

We must assume that the beginnings of Christianity in Smyrna coincided with the missionary activity of St. Paul in nearby Ephesus. From St. John's letter to the Smyrnaeans we gather that a large Jewish colony existed in Smyrna and that some Jews had embraced the Christian faith. According to the Greek *Menologion*, Apelles (Sept. 10) "who is approved in Christ" (Rom. 16:10), served as the first bishop of the church in Smyrna. Other traditions accord this honor to Ariston, who was succeeded by Strataeas, the son of Lois, who is mentioned in II Timothy 1:5. Strataeas was followed by Boucolus, who as a youth had accepted the Christian faith and later was consecrated by St. John. He may well have been the head of the church when St. John addressed the letter to the Smyrnaeans. According to the apocryphal Acts of John, St. John returned to Smyrna after his exile in Patmos.

St. John's letter to the Smyrnaeans is the most laudatory, for the writer is in full sympathy with the church. In contrast to the unemotional admiration for the Ephesians, St. John shows a keen affection for the Christians of this city, reflecting his personal knowledge of the membership.

> "And to the angel of the church in Smyrna write: 'The words of the first and the last, who died and came to life.
> " 'I know your tribulation and your poverty (but you are rich) and the slander of those who say that they are Jews and are not, but are a synagogue of Satan. Do not fear what you are about to suffer. Behold, the devil is about to throw some of you in prison, that you may be tested, and for ten days you will have tribulation. Be faithful unto death, and I will give you the crown of life. He who has an ear, let him hear what the Spirit says to the churches. He who conquers shall not be hurt by the second death.'
> Rev. 2:8-11

If any city had died through successive devastations it was Smyrna, but it had come back to life when the city was refounded by Alexander the Great. Tribulation and poverty were the problems of the church of Smyrna. The Jewish converts claimed to be the "true Israel" which, understandably, provoked a hostile reaction from the Jews of the synagogue, who informed the Roman authorities and as a result many Christians were imprisoned. We do not know where the synagogue in Smyrna was. Four Greek inscriptions of the Graeco-Roman period referring to Jews in Smyrna have been found, and one of them specifically mentions the existence of a synagogue in Smyrna.

The persecutions, however, were to last only for "ten days," though the meaning of this apocalyptic period is not clear at all. The reward for their loyalty will be "the crown of life," a metaphor the Smyrnaeans must have known well. According to the Greek philosopher Apollonius of Tyana (1st century A.D.), the phrase "the crown of Smyrna" arose from the appearance of Mount Pagus with the stately public buildings on its rounded top and the city spreading out down its rounded sloping sides. The 2nd century rhetorician Aelius Aristeides, who lived for some time in Smyrna and thought of it as the ideal city on earth, compared the city to the crown of Ariadne. St. John promises that "a new crown" shall be given to Smyrna. She shall no longer wear a mere city crown, but a crown of life. The earthly Smyrna wore a mural crown like that of her patron goddess, the celestial Smyrna shall wear a crown suited for the servants of the living God. The faithful Smyrnaeans are also not going to be hurt by "the second death, the lake of fire." (Rev. 20:14).

HISTORICAL NOTES ON THE CHURCH IN SMYRNA

In approximately 105, a few years after St. John's letter to the Smyrnaeans was written, St. Ignatius, the third bishop of Antioch-on-the-Orontes, passed through Smyrna on his way to Rome, where he was thrown to the beasts in the Roman Colosseum. His journey took him to several churches in Asia Minor and while he was in Smyrna he wrote to the Christians in Ephesus, Magnesia, Tralles, and Rome. Later on his journey, while waiting for a ship in Troy, he wrote the

Smyrnaeans and commended them for their "immovable faith as if nailed to the cross of the Lord Jesus Christ." He warned them against heretical teachers and encouraged them to obey the words of their bishops and presbyters, for "he who honors the bishop has been honored by God." He also wrote to Polycarp, the bishop of Smyrna, who had been a disciple of St. John.

St. Polycarp linked the apostolic period to the 2nd century Church. He served the church of Smyrna for nearly half a century, from 115 to 155, and throughout his life he was an uncompromising opponent of heresy. Late in his life, when he was over 80 years old, he journeyed to Rome to visit the bishop Anicetus to discuss the issue of the Easter date.

Euarestes of Smyrna recorded the trials of the martyrs of this city in a 2nd century letter sent by the church of Smyrna to the church of Philomelium (in Phrygia, near Pisidian Antioch). Eleven Christians, most of them from Philadelphia, had been brought to the Games, which were presided over by the proconsul Statius Quadratus and the asiarch Philip of Tralles. The latter praised a young man named Germanicus, who fought well against the wild beasts in the arena before they overpowered him. Another Christian, however, a Phrygian named Quintus, offered sacrifices to the gods as soon as he saw the wild beasts. The martyrdom of the other ten Christians, however, only whetted the crowd's appetite, and they cried for Polycarp. The aged bishop was arrested and prevailed upon to recant and revile Christ, but he refused, saying, "Eighty-six years I have served Him and He hath done me no wrong. How then can I speak evil of my King Who saved me?" The authorities continued their urging, but Polycarp only replied, "I am a Christian." When they heard this the crowd demanded that he be thrown to the lions immediately, but the asiarch refused since by this time the Games officially had been closed. The crowd then demanded that Polycarp be burned, and the proconsul agreed. Polycarp, "the teacher of Asia, the father of the Christians, the destroyer of the gods," met his fate with calm dignity and unflinching courage. The Christians kept his bones, which to

Here the holy Ignatius on his
to martyrdom through the cit
Smyrna is welcomed by S. Poly
the Bishop who kisseth with reve
the martyr's chains.

them were "more valuable than precious stones, and more tried than gold."

The church of Smyrna was blessed by other distinguished early Christians than St. Polycarp and St. Ignatius. St. Irenaeus, bishop of Lyons at the end of the 2nd century and one of the most distinguished theologians of the ante-Nicene church, spent his childhood in Asia Minor, probably in Smyrna, for as a child he listened to the sermons of St. Polycarp. According to a local tradition, St. Irenaeus served as an elder of the church of Smyrna. In the second part of the 2nd century the see of Smyrna was occupied by the blessed Papyrius, then by Camerius, and Thrasius of Eumenia.

During the Decian persecution (249-251) Pionius the Presbyter and his companions suffered martyrdom in Smyrna. Pionius was arrested on the anniversary of the martyrdom of Polycarp, and before he died he spoke before Polemon the temple verger.

> You men who boast of the beauty of Smyrna, and you who dwell by the river Meles and who glory in Homer, and those among this audience who are Jews, listen while I make my brief discourse. I understand that you laughed and rejoiced at those who deserted, and consider as a joke the error of those who voluntarily offered sacrifice. Men of Greece, it behoved you to listen to your teacher Homer, who counsels that it is not a holy thing to gloat over those who are to die. And as for you, men of Judaea, Moses commands, if you should see the beast of your enemy fall down under his load, you shall not pass by but you shall go and raise it up. I, at any rate, in obedience to my Master, have chosen to die rather than transgress His commands.

Euktemon, the bishop of Smyrna, apostacised and

St. Ignatius Meets St. Polycarp in Smyrna
Stained glass window in the Anglican Church of St. John, Izmir

surrendered to the demands of the government and offered sacrifices to the gods. Pionius, however, remained true to his faith and died a martyr's death.

Paganism continued to be deeply entrenched in Smyrna. In the reign of Hadrian (117-138), young men flocked for education to the colleges of Smyrna, known as "the grove of the eloquence of the sages, the museum of Ionia, the domicile of the Graces and the Muses." Pausanias, in the 2nd century, was impressed by the statues of the most exquisite workmanship of the Nemeseis and Graces who were particularly revered by the Smyrnaeans.

Our information about the church in Smyrna for the next several centuries is scanty. In 178 and again in 180 Smyrna was badly damaged by earthquakes, though each time it was rebuilt by the emperor Marcus Aurelius (161-180). In 325 Eutychius of Smyrna represented his diocese at the First Ecumenical Council in Nicaea. In the middle of the 5th century Attila the Hun conquered Smyrna, but he did not occupy the city. The Christian community grew in strength and numbers and Smyrna became one of the more important archbishoprics in Asia Minor. In 673 the city was occupied for a while by the Arabs, who were unable, however, to take the citadel. The emperor Leo the Wise (886-912) gave the church of Smyrna administrative independence as one of the major sees in the Byzantine Empire.

After the crushing defeat of the Byzantine forces at Mantzikert in 1071 the Selçuk Turks besieged Smyrna which was taken by assault in 1076 by Kutlamish Oglu Sulayman. A few years later, Tzachas, a Turkish pirate, fixed the seat of his petty emirate, which included the islands of Chios and Samos, in Smyrna. In 1097 John Ducas, brother in law of the Byzantine emperor Alexius I Comnenus, together with Admiral Caspaces, arrived in the bay of Smyrna and forced the Turks to capitulate. In the beginning of the 12th century the Byzantines restored the coastal cities which had been desolated by years of war. About Christmas time in 1147 Louis VII of France visited Smyrna on his way to Syria. During the Latin occupation of Constantinople (1204-1261) several Byzantine emperors took refuge in the region of Smyrna, particularly at Nymphaeum, today Kemalpasha, where the emperor Andronicus I (1183-1185) had built a palace. In 1222 the emperor John II Ducas Vatatzes of Nicaea (Nov. 4) rebuilt and beautified the city. After the recapture of Constantinople by the Byzantines with Genoese help, the Genoese were given trading concessions which made them virtual masters of Smyrna.

In the first few years of the 14th century the city was captured by the sultan of Aydin, although the citadel held out until 1320. A few years before the city fell a new metropolitan had been appointed to Smyrna with instructions "to lead back to the fear of God those who had been led astray, and to take in hand those who had been perverted." When the Arab traveler Ibn Batuta visited the city in 1330, Smyrna appeared to him "largely a ruined town." On October 28, 1344, the city was captured by the Knights of St. John, to whom the custody of the city had been committed by Pope Gregory XI.

In 1402 Tamerlane sent a message to the Knights summoning them to embrace Islam and threatening them with death if they refused. The Knights rejected the ultimatum and Tamerlane besieged the city, capturing it on December 17, 1402. The Knights escaped with their galleys, but the Smyrnaean Christians were massacred. When Tamerlane left he gave the city to his ally, the sultan of Aydin. Cüneyt, a prince of the sultan's family, ruled Smyrna from 1405 until 1415 when it became part of the Ottoman Empire. It was occupied briefly by the Venetians in 1472.

The Muslim occupation of Smyrna caused the church of Smyrna to lose power and prestige. In 1318 the patriarch of Constantinople had bestowed upon the metropolitan of Smyrna the bishopric of Chios "so that he might not be deprived of the necessities." We have no record of a metropolitan of Smyrna after 1389 but the church survived the conquest by Tamerlane and appears in the 15th century catalogue of metropolitan sees.

The Latin see of Smyrna was created in 1346 by Pope Clement VI and had an uninterrupted succession of titular bishops until the 17th century. The first Catholic missionaries who came to Smyrna were the Franciscans, who founded their house in 1440 near the former Greek Orthodox Cathedral of St. Photine. In 1623 the first Jesuits arrived as French consular chaplains and they were soon followed by the Capuchin fathers. The first Anglican chaplain, the Reverend Thomas Curtys, appointed by the General Court of the Levant Company, arrived in 1636, and a few years later the Dutch built a Protestant chapel in Smyrna.

One of the first Western travelers to provide us with a description of medieval Smyrna is Father Pacifique. In 1622 he listed one or two Greek churches, one small Catholic church, one synagogue, and four mosques. The Christian sites were of paramount interest for the 17th century travelers, and places associated with the ministry of St. John and the martyrdom of St. Polycarp were regularly visited. In the middle of the 17th century, "the Grotto in which St. John dwelt," near Santa Veneranda below the castle, was still pointed out, as were "the ruins of St. John's Cathedral, which has been very large and full of chapels" as well as a font used by St. John for baptisms. The Earl of Sandwich (1738) was told that the Church of St. John, converted into a mosque, was in the center of the castle, though in the beginning of the 19th century the same building was believed to have been dedicated to the Twelve Apostles. Despite the long and well established tradition of St. John's burial at Ephesus, the Smyrnaean Greeks of the 17th century took great pride in pointing out the tomb of the Apostle in Smyrna.

Yet, the most important pilgrimage site was the tomb of St. Polycarp. Father Pacifique wrote, "Where the city anciently stood, there is a petite cabane, like a hermitage, where a dervish lodges, and in this little chambrette is the coffin of St. Polycarp, not his body. It is covered with a brown cloth, and over it is placed the episcopal mitre of a curious

17th Century Smyrna
Source: Bruyn, Cornelis de, *Voyage au Levant (1674)*, Paris 1714

70

form, with Allah written in Arabic on the front of it. The Turks have much reverence for this tomb, because they say Polycarp was an evangelist of God and a friend of their Prophet Mahomet." Sieur des Hayes (1648) noted that "the Christians in Smyrna receive much consolation from the marks of sanctity which are around the city, which included the episcopal staff of St. Polycarp planted by him when he suffered martyrdom, which took root and became a cherry tree."

In 1657 the tomb of St. Polycarp was transferred from the care of the dervishes to that of the Greek monks. At that time the tomb was on the eastern side of the citadel. Richard Pococke (1739) is the first traveler to report the tomb in another location, though he reported it as being in the care of the Turks. "The spot on which the theater stood, at the foot of the hill towards the south end of the town, is all built up. One sees very little of the circus, except the foundations. At the north-west corner of the castle is the tomb of St. Polycarp. Because of great disorders committed here by the Greeks at the time of his festival, the cadi ordered a stone turban to be put on it as if it were the tomb of a Muslim saint." Gotthilf H. von Schubert (1837) added that the tomb was venerated by the Turks who here slaughtered lambs for distributing the meat to the poor in the traditional Bayram practice. Until 1952 an ecumenical service occasionally was conducted at the tomb of St. Polycarp.

Today there is no sanctuary commemorating the site of St. Polycarp's martyrdom in the stadium, but the author was shown the subterranean "prison" in the castle of Kadifekale, where tradition states that he was kept in chains. In 1655 Thevenot wrote that "below the castle, as you go to Santa Veneranda, which is a church of the Greeks, there is a great amphitheater, where St. Polycarp suffered martyrdom. It is very high, and in the upper part thereof, there are still five niches, where the seats of the magistrates were." Neither the amphitheater (stadium) on the western nor the remains of the theater on the northwestern slope of Mount Pagus have survived. In 1675 the theater was destroyed by the vizier

Ahmad who used the materials to construct other buildings. The stadium of Smyrna, the site of St. Polycarp's martyrdom, was about a quarter of a mile west of the castle, close to the modern road leading up to the castle. One can still identify a long hollow, which now, however, is completely built over.

In 1688 there was a severe earthquake in Smyrna which killed 4,000 people. In 1694 the Venetians captured the island of Chios, and shortly afterwards Venetian galleys appeared in the Gulf of Smyrna. The Turks prepared to take all Christians in Smyrna as hostages, but the British, French, and Dutch consuls persuaded the Venetians to withdraw. In 1770 Russia called on the Greeks to revolt and the Turks took revenge, killing more than 10,000 Greeks in Smyrna alone. Twenty-seven years later a large fire raged through Smyrna reducing 4,500 homes to ashes.

Throughout these difficult centuries the Christian community in Smyrna, reminded by the apostolic exhortation "to be faithful unto death and to receive the crown of life," fearlessly continued in its witness. It is impossible to list the names of all the Christians of this city, who, following the example of St. Polycarp, laid down their lives for their commitment to Christ, but many are commemorated by the Greek Orthodox Church. Most of these "New Martyrs" were poor people who had embraced Islam for various reasons, but later repented and publicly proclaimed their faith in Jesus Christ. Athanasius of Attalia (Jan. 7), who lived most of his life in Smyrna, was said to have embraced Islam, but in 1653 when he returned to his Christian faith he was decapitated. In 1675 Nicholas of Karaman (Dec. 6), in a moment of anger, swore he would become a Muslim, and when he refused to fulfill this oath he was hanged. Dioscorus of Smyrna (May 11) experienced a similar fate. Demus of Smyrna (April 10) was accused by his Turkish master of insulting Islam and was beheaded in 1763. Alexander of Salonica (May 26) had even become a hodja, but as he preached the crucified Christ he was martyred in Smyrna in 1794. Other New Martyrs of Smyrna include Procopius the New Martyr (June 25), who was killed in 1810; Agathangelus the New Martyr (April 19), who suffered martyrdom in 1818; and Nektarius the New Martyr (July 11) who was hanged in 1820.

Smyrna is said to have had between 10,000 and 12,000 Christians in the 17th century, but only two churches. In 1739 Richard Pococke estimated 7,000 to 8,000 Greeks with three churches, 2,000 Armenians with one church, and 5,000 to 6,000 Jews with one synagogue. In the beginning of the 19th century, Gregory, the metropolitan of Smyrna, was enthroned patriarch of Constantinople where, in 1821 at the start of the successful Greek revolt for independence from Turkish rule, he was hanged from the gateway of the patriarchate. His relics repose in the Cathedral of the Annunciation in Athens. When A.S. Noroff visited Smyrna in the middle of the 19th century there were 40,000 Greeks with seven churches in the city, A few years later F.V.J. Arundell saw two Latin and two Protestant churches and one Anglican and one Dutch church.

The first Protestant missionaries arrived in Smyrna in the first quarter of the 19th century. The Reverend Charles Williamson of the Church of England (CMS) settled in the city in 1817, followed in 1820 by the Revds. Pliny Fisk and Levi Parsons of the American Board of Commissioners for Foreign Missions. Soon other American missionaries arrived, and in 1823 the Bible Society established in Smyrna a center for missionary work in the Levant. In 1878 the American Collegiate Institute was founded in Smyrna. The college functioned until the upheavals of 1922, when its buildings were burned down. Miss Emily McCullum reestablished one section in Athens, now known as Pierce College, while Miss Olive Greene moved her section to Göztepe, the present site of the Amerikan Kiz Koleji. In 1902, the American Board founded International College in the Smyrna suburb of Buca (Paradise), where it remained until 1934 when it was moved to Beirut. The imposing buildings of the Buca campus are now used by NATO. For the missionaries of the American Board, Smyrna was a major center through which they supplied mumerous smaller stations in Western Turkey. In the middle of the 19th century the German Evangelical

Church in Smyrna was established to serve the German speaking Protestants. It was assisted by the Evangelical Kaiserswerth deaconesses, who maintained a school, hospital, and orphanage under the leadership of Sister Minna Grosse.

In 1906 Smyrna was a predominantly Christian city with 135,000 Greeks, 11,175 Catholics, 8,500 Armenians, 91,885 Muslims, 25,500 Jews, and 2,860 others. The Greek Orthodox Metropolitan Cathedral was dedicated to St. Photine the Samaritan Woman, and other churches were named after saints Catherine, George, Demetrius, John the Theologian, Constantine, Nicholas, Tryphon, Michael, Anne, and there were churches dedicated to the Nativity of the Holy Virgin, the Transfiguration, and the Panagia Myrtidiotissa. In all, the Greeks maintained 55 churches and 133 priests in and around Smyrna. One of the most beautiful churches until the devastation of 1922 was the Armenian Cathedral of St. Stephen, built early in the 20th century.

After the First World War Greece laid claim to the Smyrna area, and the decision of the Council of Three authorizing the Greeks to occupy Smyrna apparently was taken without the knowledge of the Italians and the Americans. On May 15, 1919, Greek troops occupied Smyrna and, according to the Treaty of Sèvres signed on August 10, 1920, Smyrna and the Ionian hinterland were placed for five years under Greek administration. This was unacceptable to the young state of Turkey, and Turkish forces under Mustafa Kemal began opposing the Greek presence. Negotiations at the London and Paris conferences failed and the Turks drove back the overextended Greek forces. The Turkish army entered Smyrna on September 9, 1922 and soon thereafter the city went up in flames. On September 15, Chrysostomus, Metropolitan of Smyrna, suffered martyrdom. The metropolitan of Ephesus escaped in disguise on board a foreign vessel. A fire razed most of the Armenian quarter. It is estimated that 50,000 Christians were killed in the city during this period. No indigenous Christians remained in Smyrna after this holocaust which has deeply strained relations between the two peoples. Perhaps the first real understanding of this tragedy was shown by the great British historian, Arnold Toynbee, who placed the blame squarely on the shoulders of the western statesmen, Lloyd George in particular, who supported the Greek claim to Anatolian territory.

CHRISTIAN CHURCHES AND RUINS IN SMYRNA

Izmir is the only city of the Seven Churches of the Apocalypse in which Christians still regularly assemble for worship. In the Roman Catholic Cathedral of St. John the Evangelist, built in 1862 by Archbishop Vincent Spaccapietra, Apostolic Delegate to Asia Minor, Catholics and

Izmir: Catholic Cathedral of St. John the Evangelist

Protestants, most of them foreigners, worship every Sunday. This church, adorned with many 19th century paintings of SS. John, Polycarp, Ignatius, Irenaeus, and others, was granted by Pope Pius IX the high honor of being a Minor Basilica, enriched with the same indulgences as that of St. John Lateran in Rome. The Cathedral is at Shehit Nevres Bulvari. The Roman Catholics maintain eight other churches and chapels in Izmir.

The Anglican Church of St. John the Evangelist at Alsancak, built in 1898 on the site of the former chapel of the Levant Company, provides regular Sunday services, and occasional services are held in the Anglican churches in Bornova (St. Mary Magdalene) and Buca (All Saints).

The Greek Orthodox community serving with the NATO forces in Izmir has worshiped since the early fifties in the Dutch Chapel, which the Greek Orthodox Church leased from the Dutch Reformed Church for 99 years. The chapel, now dedicated to St. Photine in commemoration of the former Greek Orthodox Cathedral of Smyrna, is at number 24 on 1324 Street, Alsancak.

A few scattered remains of a former Byzantine church (or churches) of Smyrna can be seen among the marble fragments in the Hellenic-Roman Agora of ancient Smyrna.

Izmir: Marble Fragment from a 6th Century Church
In the Temple of Athena Polias Nikephoros, Agora

To the Church in Pergamum

ON ANCIENT PERGAMUM

Ceramic works uncovered in the region of Pergamum indicate that a small settlement may have existed on the present site of the town in the Archaic period. Pergamum was ruled by a Persian viceroy, Gongylus, during the height of the Persian expansion. Greek mercenaries later led by Xenophon passed through the town in 400-399 B.C. on their way to support the unsuccessful revolt of Cyrus the Younger against his brother Artaxerxes II of Persia. After the death of Alexander the Great in 333 B.C., Lysimachus, one of Alexander's generals, gained control of western Asia Minor. He desposited 9,000 talents in Pergamum for safekeeping and appointed a Paphlagonian eunuch named Philetaerus to guard the treasure. When Lysimachus was killed in 281 B.C. the country fell to the Seleucid kingdom, but Philetaerus retained control of Pergamum and the treasure, with which he founded the Pergamene monarchy. Eumenes (263-241 B.C.), the adopted son and successor of Philetaerus, became the first king of Pergamum. The city thrived and for 150 years, from 283 to 133 B.C., was one of the most brilliant cultural centers of the Hellenistic world. According to Livy (57 B.C. - 17 A.D) the kingdom of Pergamum was founded on brotherly harmony, because "one brother wore the name of king, but all brothers ruled." When Attalus III of Pergamum died in 133 B.C., he bequeathed the kingdom to the Roman Empire. The Romans proclaimed the area the province of Asia with Pergamum its capital.

The Attalids, as the later Pergamene kings were called, were the most outstanding bibliophiles of the ancient world. Eumenes II (197-159 B.C.) and Attalus II (159-138 B.C.) had

Reconstruction Drawing of the Upper City of Pergamum (Koch, 1886)
Source: *Chronik der Ausgrabung von Pergamum 1871-1886.* Dortmund, 1963

books of all kinds brought to Pergamum. The 2nd century A.D. physician, Galen of Pergamum, mentions that manuscripts were even forged to satisfy the kings' desire for more and more books. The Pergamene library is said to have totalled 200,000 volumes, rivalling the Alexandrian library. The 1st century B.C. Roman writer Marcus T. Varro, who lived in Pergamum, reports that Ptolemy prohibited the export of papyrus in order to stem the growth of the Pergamene collection. The Pergamenes resorted to the use of skins for writing, and from their *charta pergamena* we derive our word parchment. The Pergamene collection was eventually given by Anthony to Cleopatra, but we cannot be certain that it ever reached Alexandria.

The Asklepium in Pergamum was as important a medical center in the Roman Empire as were the asklepia of Cos and Epidaurus. The patient slept in the sanctuary and either awoke cured or related his dreams to the priests who prescribed treatment according to the dreams. This method is often referred to as therapy by incubation. In 215 A.D., however, when the emperor Caracalla visited the Asklepium for treatment, the god of healing was unmoved by the imperial supplications. Galen (ca. 130-200 A.D.), the most famous physician of antiquity after Hippocrates, was born in Pergamum.

APOSTOLIC PERGAMUM

In the 1st century A.D. Pergamum, with its famous temples of Zeus Soter, Dionysus, and Athena, was the principal center of the imperial cult in the province of Asia. Here were the temples of the emperor Augustus and the goddess Roma, with their cult statues to which everyone had to pay homage. Confrontation between the young Christian church of Pergamum and the state was inevitable. We do not know when Christianity found its way to Pergamum, though we must assume that a local congregation existed in the second half of the 1st century. According to the *Apostolic Constitutions*, the "beloved Gaius" whom John the Elder addressed in his Third Letter, was the first bishop of

Pergamum. Gaius was followed by Antipas, believed by some people to have been a dentist, who died a martyr. Some scholars have felt that the name was symbolical, and is formed of two Greek words, in imitation of the anti-Christ, meaning one who stands firm in the faith "against all" (ἀντὶ πᾶς) trials and enemies.

St. John fully acknowledged the difficulties the Pergamene church faced.

> "And to the angel of the church in Pergamum write:
> 'The words of him who has the sharp two-edged sword.
> " 'I know where you dwell, where Satan's throne is; you hold fast my name and you did not deny my faith even in the days of Antipas my witness, my faithful one, who was killed among you, where Satan dwells. But I have a few things against you: you have some there who hold the teaching of Balaam, who taught Balak to put a stumbling block before the sons of Israel, that they might eat food sacrificed to idols and practice immorality. So you also have some who hold the teaching of the Nicolaitans. Repent then. If not, I will come to you soon and war against them with the sword of my mouth. He who has an ear, let him hear what the Spirit says to the churches. To him who conquers I will give some of the hidden manna, and I will give him a white stone, with a new name written on the stone which no one knows except him who receives it.'
> Rev. 2:12-17

Of the Seven Churches addressed by St. John, the two churches of Pergamum and Thyatira are treated with mingled praise and blame, though on the whole praise outweighs the blame. In the opening sentence Christ is represented as having the two-edged sword. The *ius gladii,* the right of the sword, was the power over life and death, which the Romans of the province believed to be vested in the proconsul. Here, this right is assumed by Christ. In the reference to "Satan's Throne" some scholars have seen an allusion to the great altar of Zeus Soter which was erected on a hill almost 800 feet above the city. The altar, now in the Pergamon Museum in East Berlin, was built by Eumenes II and adorned with reliefs representing the battle of the gods and giants, symbolizing the victory of Eumenes I over the Galatians early in the 3rd century B.C.

Other scholars, such as Johann Weiss and Florence Banks, have identified "Satan's Throne" either with the Asklepium in general or the mystical cyst kept in the Asklepium. This mystical cyst was a chest in which was kept a live serpent, a special object of veneration for all believers in Asklepius. St. John, however, was more concerned with the idolatry of emperor worship than with the established Hellenic cults. It is much more likely, therefore, that he thought of "Satan's Throne" either as the preeminent Asian temple of the divine Augustus or as the imperial cult in general, in which he saw the incarnation of Satan. At any rate, he praises the Pergamene Christians for maintaining their faith in the principal seat of the imperial cult. Despite their

The Altar of Zeus, Pergamum
Pergamon Museum, Berlin

loyalty to Christ and the fearless witness of Antipas, some Pergamene Christians were holding to the heresy of Balaam, who had caused Balak to induce the Israelites to "eat food sacrificed to idols and practice immorality." The main passage concerning Balaam is found in Numbers 22-24. According to Jewish tradition Balaam was identified with idolatry and temple prostitution. The question of eating meat sacrificed to idols also had arisen in Corinth, and St. Paul had admonished the Corinthians not to eat of such food (1 Cor. 10:14-22).

St. John clearly recognized the threat to unity and the apostolic faith from these people. As a true shepherd he admonished the wavering Christians to repent, for otherwise Christ will war against them with the sword of His mouth. On the other hand, those adhering to the apostolic faith are promised certain rewards. Just as the Israelites were fed manna on their journey to the Promised Land, so the faithful Christians will be rewarded for their loyalty with spiritual manna. Each loyal believer also will receive a white stone and a new name, probably written on a kind of phylactery to protect him and to assure his immortality.

We must assume that in Pergamum as elsewhere the Christian community included some Hellenistic Jewish converts. Again we do not know where the synagogue was, although a gable from a synagogue door or screen of the Graeco-Roman period showing a menorah has been discovered in Pergamum.

HISTORICAL NOTES ON THE CHURCH
IN PERGAMUM

Heresies continued in Pergamum and, in the middle of the 2nd century, Bishop Theodotus of Pergamum was forced to condemn the heretic Colorbasius. Political pressure upon the church also continued. During the Decian persecutions (249-251) the martyrs included Carpus, bishop of Thyatira; Papylus, the deacon of Thyatira; Agathodorus; and a woman named Agathonike who died, according to Eusebius, "after many glorious confessions" (Oct. 13).

In 347, Eusebius, bishop of Pergamum, attended the

Synod of Sardica (Sofia), which reaffirmed previous disciplinary canons and assigned the bishop of Rome as the court of appeal for accused prelates. Bishop Dracontius of Pergamum participated in the synodical debates in Constantinople in 360. In 431, Philip of Pergamum represented his diocese at the Third Ecumenical Council in Ephesus. From the middle of the 5th century on, the church of Pergamum sided with the Alexandrians in their anti-Roman and anti-Byzantine policies. At the infamous Robber Council of Ephesus in 449, Eutropius of Pergamum accepted the Eutychian doctrines which stated that Christ had only one nature, that of the incarnate Word, and for the following years Pergamum remained a center of Eutychianism, an extreme form of Monophysitism. In the latter part of the 6th century the city attracted an ever increasing number of Armenians, partly on account of its anti-Roman theological posture. The most famous Pergamene Armenian was Bardanes, better known as Philippicus, who became a distinguished general under Justinian II and emperor himself for two years (711-713) after Justinian II was assassinated.

In 716-717 Pergamum was besieged by Maslamah, brother of the caliph Sulayman. The defenders were told by a magician that they could save the city by dipping their right hands in a cauldron in which an unborn child cut from its mother's womb had been boiled. The Greek chronicler Theophanes the Confessor (758-818) blames the fall of the city to the Arabs on the elders who performed this grisly ritual.

The town never fully recovered from the devastation wrought by the troops of Maslamah. In the 10th century Pergamum was listed as less important than Thyatira, Miletus, and Priene. For a time Pergamum was attached to the province of Samos. In the 13th century, during the reign of the Comneni emperors, it experienced a brief renaissance and became the capital of the province of Neokastra. From 1211 until 1214 the Latin emperor of Constantinople, Henry of Flanders, occupied Pergamum, after which it came under the control of the Byzantine Empire of Nicaea. In 1250 the Byzantine emperor Theodore II Lascaris visited Pergamum and, in a letter to the historian Georgios Akropolites, described his impressions of the destroyed theaters and the house of the physician Galen which was especially pointed out to him. In 1330, when the Arab traveler Ibn Batuta visited Pergamum, the house of Galen was known as the house of Plato. Ibn Batuta described Pergamum as a ruined city with a large fortress on top of a hill.

Early in the 14th century Pergamum fell under Turkish rule. By 1336 it was controlled by the Ottoman Turks and, except for a short occupation in 1402 by Tamerlane who massacred the population, the city remained in Ottoman hands. By the time of the patriarchate of Nilus (1380-1388), the Christian community in Pergamum had decreased so much in size and strength that it could no longer support a priest, and the church was attached to the metropolitan see of Ephesus. In 1398 Sultan Bayazid I transformed the Church of Haghia Sophia into the Ulu Çamii, or Grand Mosque. When Cyriacus of Ancona visited Pergamum in 1431 and 1444 he did not mention the Christian community and only referred to the theater and the amphitheater. There was some vitality in the Pergamum church a century later, for the Byzantine Christians rebuilt the Church of St. Theodore in 1545.

Even after the fall of Constantinople in 1453 to the Ottomans, Christians throughout Asia Minor retained their faith in the effective opposition of their saints and sanctuaries to Ottoman rule. Mosques which had served as churches were considered hostile to Muslims. In Pergamum the Church of St. John, the so-called Red Basilica, was turned into a mosque; its door was believed to have "turned northward" and its minaret to have collapsed. A cross is said to have appeared on the Church of Haghia Sophia after its conversion into a mosque.

The interest in Pergamum as one of the Seven Churches begins with the European travelers of the 17th century. In addition to a detailed description of the Church of St. John, Thomas Smith in 1671 wrote of "a very handsome large church, formerly called Sancta Sophia, into which you ascend by several stone stairs, now polluted by the Turks and made a Mosque." As in the 1st century the Pergamenes practised idolatry and immorality, in the 17th century they were reported by Paul Rycaut (1675) to "addict themselves principally to thefts and robberies." Furthermore, Rycaut observed that the city had decayed very rapidly, "so that whereas ten years ago there were fifty-three streets of this town inhabited, there are now only twenty-two frequented, the others are deserted." The Christian community in Pergamum persisted in identifying the Grand Mosque or Ulu Çamii as the Church of Haghia Sophia, although the transformation was made in 1398. F.V.J. Arundell (1826) was told that the church was converted into a mosque in 1810 and Gotthilf H. von Schubert (1836) heard that the relics of St. Antipas used to repose in the Church of Haghia Sophia. The Reverend H. Christmas (1851) called it the Mosque of Haghia Sophia and reported that it was believed to have been the church in which the Christians assembled when they received the letter by St. John. He also was told that the mosque contained the tomb of St. Antipas, who suffered martyrdom by being burned in a brazen bull.

By the 17th century the Church of St. John was in ruins. F.V.J. Arundell mentioned that this church was converted into a mosque soon after the capture of Constantinople by the Turks, and that a minaret was built on its northeast end. The Muslims, however, refused to use the mosque "because of a miraculous change of position of the door of this minaret." One of the circular rooms appeared to have been used as a church, for Arundell saw "a dirty lamp hanging before some wretched paper saint." Today the ground floor of the north tower is used as a mosque.

In the 17th century the only active church in Pergamum, dedicated to St. Theodore, served only some twelve to fifteen

Bergama: Kizli Avlu or Red Basilica

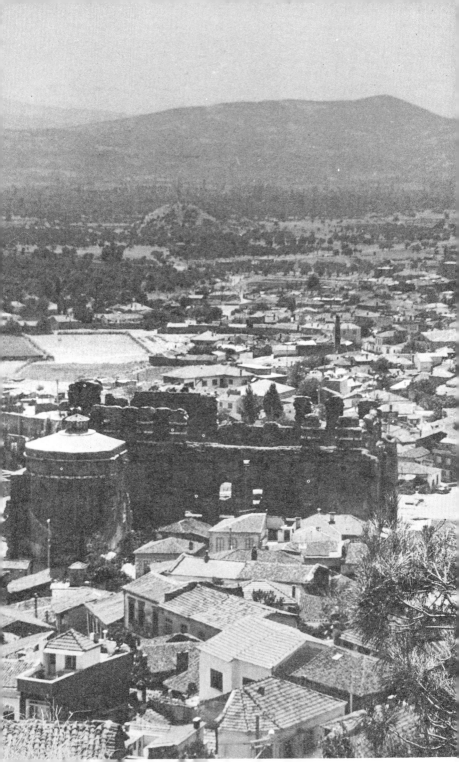

families, but in 1826 F.V.J. Arundell reported 1,500 Greeks, 200 Armenians, and 100 Jews in the city. A.S. Noroff (1860) wrote of 200 Greek and 25 Armenian homes. The Greek church was on the ascent to the acropolis and, according to F.V.J. Arundell, it was "a poor shed covered with earth." Next to it the Greeks maintained a small school with thirty pupils. Before the First World War the Christians possessed four churches in Pergamum; the Metropolitan Church of St. Theodore and the churches of St. John the Theologian, St. Antipas, and St. Paraskeve.

Archaeological work in Pergamum began late in the 19th century. Carl Humann's discovery of the high reliefs of the altar of Zeus incorporated into the Byzantine wall led the way to the excavation of the ancient city. The first excavations (1878-1886) under Carl Humann, Alexander Conze, and R. Bohn unearthed the upper city. Later (1900-1913) W. Dörpfeld directed the excavations of the middle and lower districts of the city. In the third excavation period (1927-1936) Theodor Wiegand excavated the arsenals, the so-called Red Basilica (The Church of St. John), and the Asklepium. In 1957 the excavations in Pergamum were resumed and work is now being extended to all parts of the city.

CHRISTIAN RUINS IN PERGAMUM

Archaeologists have excavated four churches in Pergamum. The remains do not permit us to assign precise dates, but we may assume that the original buildings belong to the pre-Arab period. The best known church, the so-called Red Basilica or Kizil Avlu, traditionally identified with St. John, was built on the ruins of a temple. This temple was the largest building in ancient Pergamum and was dedicated to the Egyptian god Serapis. Some material from the temple was used in the construction of the Christian basilica. It was destroyed by the Arabs in 716-717 and later rebuilt. Another church with two aisles was excavated by W. Dörpfeld in the courtyard of the lower agora, but no remains of this church are visible today. A church approximately 15 m. long and 5.50 m. wide was built during the Justinian period (527-65) on the site of the Temple of Athena on the acropolis; a few marble fragments of this church may be seen *in situ.* Ruins of the fourth church were found on the terrace of the Pergamene theater, but no traces of them remain.

Bergama: Marble Fragment from a 6th Century Church
In the Temple of Athena, Acropolis

To the Church in Thyatira

ON ANCIENT THYATIRA

According to the 6th century geographer Stephen of Byzantium, Thyatira was given its name by Seleucus I Nicator (312-281 B.C.), and the name probably is of Lydian origin. Strabo mentions that Thyatira was a Macedonian colony known as "the farthermost city of the Mysians," and Pliny informs us that the city previously had been called Pelopian or Euhippian Thyatira. Here Antiochus III established his headquarters before his defeat at Magnesia in 190 B.C. by the Romans commanded by Scipio Africanus. After his surrender Thyatira became part of the kingdom of Pergamum and, in 133 B.C., a Roman possession. Asklepius, Dionysus, and Artemis were worshiped in Thyatira, and the sun god Apollo Tyrimnaios was the city's tutelary divinity. Apollo's worship was joined with that of the emperor who was identified as Apollo incarnate and, like him, the son of Zeus.

The city was strategically situated on the main road to Pergamum from the east, which passed through Apameia, Laodicea, and Philadelphia as well as Thyatira. Thyatira's geographical location was different from that of the other six cities to which St. John wrote. The ancient city was built on only slightly elevated ground. Unlike Ephesus, Smyrna, Pergamum, Sardis, Philadelphia, and Laodicea, nature had provided Thyatira with no natural fortress. This is fundamental to our understanding of the history of this city for, without any geographical aids for its defense, it was the first target for any invader from the east who sought to conquer Pergamum, which kept a strong military garrison in Thyatira. "Its history was that of a sentinal town," Vernon P. Flynn pointed out, "its fate to be overrun, destroyed and

Akhisar: View of the Town from the Minaret of the Sheyhisa Çamii rebuilt." This experience may well have determined the collective character of its citizens, for a city which repeatedly was passed from ruler to ruler must have developed either a feeling of futility or a capacity to shift loyalties easily.

APOSTOLIC THYATIRA

The first Thyatiran Christian, though a resident of Philippi in Macedonia,

> was a woman named Lydia . . . a seller of purple goods, who was a worshiper of God. The Lord opened her heart to give heed to what was said by Paul. And when she was baptized, with her household, she besought us, saying, "If you have judged me to be faithful to the Lord, come to my house and stay." And she prevailed upon us.
>
> Acts 16:14-15

Akhisar: 2nd Century Road and Stoa of Thyatira
Tepe Mezari

Since Lydia was a householder and her husband is not mentioned, we assume she was a widow. The reference to her as a believer in God suggests that she may have accepted the Jewish faith in Thyatira where there was a Jewish colony. Lydia was not the only representative of her trade in Philippi. In 1872 Professor Mertzides discovered in Philippi the following text in Greek inscribed on a piece of white marble: "The city honored from among the purple dyers, an outstanding citizen, Antiochus, the son of Lykus, a native of Thyatira, as a benefactor." The purple dyers of Thyatira may have had representatives in Philippi, where their profession seems to have been held in high esteem. From Thyatiran coins we know that Thyatira was the home of many respected guilds, such as tanners, coppersmiths, potters, linen weavers, wool workers, bakers, and bronzesmiths.

We know almost nothing of the foundation of the Christian Church in Thyatira. We must assume, however, that by the second half of the 1st century a Christian community existed in this city, for the threat of internal dissension and schism mentioned in St. John's letter presupposes some formal organization.

St. John's letter to the church in Thyatira, the longest of the Seven Letters, praises, admonishes, and promises rewards as does the letter to the church in Pergamum.

"And to the angel of the church of Thyatira write: 'The words of the Son of God, who has eyes like a flame of fire, and whose feet are like burnished bronze.

" 'I know your works, your love and faith and service and patient endurance, and that your latter works exceed the first. But I have this against you, that you tolerate the woman Jezebel, who calls herself a prophetess and is teaching and beguiling my servants to practice immorality and to eat food sacrificed to idols. I gave her time to repent, but she refuses to repent of her immorality. Behold I will throw her on a sickbed, and those who commit adultery with her I will throw into great tribulation, unless they repent of her doings; and I will strike her children dead. And all the churches shall know that I am he who searches mind and heart, and I will give to each of you as your works deserve. But to the rest of you in Thyatira, who do not hold this teaching, who have not learned what some call the deep things of Satan, to you I say, I do not lay upon you any other burden; only hold fast what you have, until I come. He who conquers and keeps my words until the end, I will give him power over the nations, and he shall rule them with a rod of iron, as when earthen pots are broken in pieces, even as I myself have received power from my Father; and I will give him the morning star. He who has an ear, let him hear what the Spirit says to the churches.'

Rev. 2:18-29

St. John contrasts the local pagan imagery of the emperor-Apollo with the celestial Christ with eyes like a flame of fire and His feet like burnished bronze. Worship of the emperor as the incarnate Apollo, the son of Zeus, is set against the worship of the Son of God. The reference to burnished bronze is particularly fitting, for Thyatira was well known for its bronzesmiths. Florence A. Banks published a Thyatiran coin showing a bronzesmith seated at an anvil and delivering the finishing blow with a hammer to a helmet, while Athena, standing nearby, holds out her hand to receive the helmet.

St. John commends the Thyatiran Christians for their patient endurance of persecution, but he follows praise with blame for tolerating "the woman Jezebel," who had led many members of the church of Thyatira to practise immorality and eat food sacrificed to idols. Just as the ancient Jezebel, the notorious wife of the Old Testament king Ahab, had introduced the worship of alien gods in Israel (I Kings 16 - 21), this Thyatiran Jezebel had led the Christians of Thyatira to repeat the sins for which St. Paul had rebuked the Corinthians: "It is actually reported that there is immorality among you . . . And you are arrogant! Ought you not rather to mourn?" (I Cor. 5:1). This lady apparently was widely accepted in Thyatira as a prophetess. She must have been active and vocal to succeed in turning some members of the young church back to the idolatry of pagan cults. St. John considers the lack of opposition to her as the principal fault of the whole congregation. Some scholars have suggested that she was connected with a particular cult, but it seems unlikely that she was a priestess of the temple of the Chaldaean Sibyl in Thyatira, where pagan and Jewish rites were practised.

Despite this lady's success, not all Thyatiran Christians had followed her teachings, and the church was split on the issue. Those who had not learned the "deep things of Satan" as promulgated by this prophetess are reminded to remain loyal and devoted until Christ Himself shall come. The faithful are promised "power over nations" and "the morning star." The first reference, an allusion to Psalm 2:8-9, portrays the image of a victorious Christ, Who will rule the conquered nations "with a rod of iron" (Rev. 12:5). St. John envisages Christ ruling nations assisted by the martyrs of His church, dressed in white linen and riding white horses. The gift of the morning star is the gift of life and immortality. As the evening star, the goddess Ishtar, signified death, so "the bright morning star," Christ Himself (Rev. 22:16), is the gift of eternal life to the loyal Christians of Thyatira. St. John expresses unhesitating and sublime confidence in the victory of the believer.

HISTORICAL NOTES ON THE CHURCH IN THYATIRA
We know very little about the history of this community which was to receive "power over nations." The city was visited by the emperors Hadrian in 123 A.D. and Caracalla in 215 A.D. Caracalla made a number of urban improvements and received the title Benefactor of Thyatira. In the middle of the 3rd century Carpus, Bishop of Thyatira, Papylus his deacon, and two other, presumably Thyatiran, Christians were taken to Pergamum where they suffered martyrdom (Oct. 13). According to St. Epiphanius, the 4th century bishop of Constantia in Cyprus, the church of Thyatira had embraced the Montanist heresy by the middle of the 3rd

century. Montanism was an ecstatic and eschatologically oriented movement which drew its inspiration chiefly from the Johannine writings, and it is probable that Montanist reverence for the Book of Revelation was the main reason for the late admission of this book to the canon of Holy Scriptures in the Eastern Church. Thyatira sent its Bishop Sozon to the first Ecumenical Council of Nicaea in 325, and its Bishop Fuscus to the Council of Ephesus in 431. The history of the Thyatiran church for the next several centuries roughly parallels the history of the church in Sardis. As late as the 10th century the diocese of Thyatira was suffragan to Sardis.

In 1313 Thyatira was occupied by Sarukhan, the emir of Manisa (Magnesia ad-Sipylum). In 1425 the plain of Thyatira was the scene of a battle against Cüneyt Bey, a Turkish adventurer. After his defeat, the city fell to the Ottomans and became part of their empire, and the name Akhisar meaning "white castle" replaced the old name Thyatira. During the Ottoman period Akhisar became a major center for the cotton industry.

The ancient name was not associated with Akhisar until late in the 17th century. One of the first Westerners to visit Akhisar was the Reverend Thomas Smith who, on April 3, 1671, set out from Smyrna with eleven companions, including a cook and three grooms, for "the roads were infested with robbers in strong and numerous parties well mounted and armed." Smith found eight mosques in Akhisar, but no traces of a church. Two years later, Pickering and Salter visited Akhisar and were equally unsuccessful in locating traces of a church. In 1675, Sir Paul Rycaut, the English consul in Smyrna, discovered the name Thyatira on an ancient inscription on the base of a pillar in the Akhisar market. He found no more than ten Christians in the town and the name Thyatira unknown, but he was shown a small mosque which had been built as a church. Several times the minaret of this mosque had fallen down. George Wheler, probably using second hand information, wrote that "the reason they (the people of Thyatira) give, is, that it having been a Christian church, God will not suffer it to stand. For it

96

has been several times built or set up, and as often suddenly thrown down." As in the case of the mosque in Pergamum, the Muslims of Akhisar attributed the collapse of the minaret to the anti-Islamic influence resident in the mosque.

J. Aegidius van Egmont passed through Akhisar in 1759, but reported only that the inhabitants subsisted entirely by the cultivation of cotton. Richard Chandler, who traveled in the area in 1764, did not go to Akhisar because a Greek priest had informed one of Chandler's companions "that he had recent intelligence from Thyatira and that the plague was in the house of the Aga." During the 18th and early 19th centuries Greeks and Armenians moved to and settled in Akhisar. F.V.J. Arundell, the Anglican chaplain of Smyrna, visited the town in 1826 and left the following report: "The appearance of Thyatira as we approached it was that of a long line of cypresses, poplars and other trees, amidst which appeared the minarets of several mosques and the roofs of a few houses. Thyatira is a large place and abounds with shops." He was told that there were 1,000 Turkish, 300 Greek and 30 Armenian families. The Greeks maintained one church, "a wretchedly poor place, and so much under the level of the church-yard, as to require five steps to descend to it." The priest, who spoke only Turkish, told him that the bishop of Ephesus was the "archierefs" (Greek for bishop) of Thyatira. Charles Fellows and Charles G. Addison, though traveling separately, both visited the town in or around 1838 and noticed fragments of the ancient city used in the contemporary houses. "This town teems with relics of a former splendid city, although there is not a trace of the site of any ruins or early buildings. I saw ten or a dozen well-tops or troughs made of the capitals of columns of different kinds . . . The streets in places are paved with fragments of carved stone." Charles Addison noted that the roof of the large khan was supported by ancient marble columns.

In 1832 the Greeks built the Cathedral of St. Nicholas. The older church was named after the 3rd century bishop of Thyatira and his deacon, SS. Carpus and Papylus. In 1854 the Smyrna Station of the Western Turkey Mission of the

American Board for Commissioners of Foreign Missions established an outstation and school in Akhisar where Greek and Armenian Evangelical pastors served until 1922. Shortly before the First World War there were 22,000 people living in and around Akhisar: 11,000 Turks; 12,000 Greeks; 800 Armenians; 150 Jews. As was Smyrna, Akhisar was the scene of many tragedies in 1922. On August 28, 1922, the Greek mayor of Akhisar advised all the Greeks to leave, but many refused to go. A few days later, Akhisar was occupied by the advancing Turkish troops, and an estimated 7,000 Greek Greek Christians were killed.

There has been no Christian community in Akhisar since 1922, but the Greek Orthodox Archbishop of Great Britain carries the title of Metropolitan of Thyatira. He resides at Thyatira House, 5 Craven Hill, London, W.2. The remaining six abandoned Apostolic sees in Asia Minor are occasionally bestowed as titular sees upon members of the Holy Synod of the Ecumenical Patriarchate of Constantinople.

CHRISTIAN RUINS IN THYATIRA

Akhisar today is a thriving Turkish town — its 1973 population was 47,850 — with few traces of its vanished Christian community. The 19th century Cathedral of St. Nicholas has been converted into a movie theater. In the inner court of the Ulu Çamii or Grand Mosque of Akhisar, immediately to the east of the building, are the foundations of a large apse of an early Byzantine church. The size of the foundations indicates that this must have been a large church, and a local tradition, still upheld by the hodja of the mosque, maintains that the Ulu Çamii was built on the site of the Church of St. Basil. Inside the mosque are several 10th century alabaster columns which are also believed to have belonged to the Church of St. Basil.

According to another local tradition, the Sheyhisa Çamii (Sheikh Jesus Mosque) was first built as the Church of St.

Akhisar: Foundation Walls of Apse of Byzantine Church
Courtyard, Ulu Çamii

John the Theologian. In the outer court of the mosque are two Corinthian capitals which may have belonged to the former church but there is no other architectural or archaeological evidence to support this tradition.

Before the First World War, remains of churches, primarily marble slabs with cross designs, were stored in the courtyard of the Cathedral of St. Nicholas. A marble slab with the imperial eagle used to be in the residence of Mr. M. Kachajas, a prominent Greek theologian in Akhisar early in the 20th century. Today, several remains of Christian churches of Thyatira are exhibited in the Archaeological Museum in Manisa.

Recent excavations at Tepe Mezari in the center of Akhisar, which have unearthed a section of a 2nd century A.D. Roman road and part of a stoa as well as the walls of a 6th century administrative building (?), may also reveal ruins of Christian buildings, throwing additional light upon the early Christian heritage of this city.

Marble Slab with Byzantine Eagle, from Thyatira

Source: Josef Keil und Anton von Premerstein, *Bericht über eine Zweite Reise in Lydien.* Wien, 1911

Fragment of an Altar Screen from a Byzantine Church in
Thyatira
Archaeological Museum, Manisa

To the Church in Sardis

ON ANCIENT SARDIS

According to Homer, the ancient capital of the Hermus Valley at the foot of Mount Tmolous, the birthplace of Dionysus, was known as Hyde. This city, protected by its powerful acropolis and watered by the small Pactolus River, became the capital of the ancient kingdom of Lydia. Herodotus (1:7 ff), informs us that the kingship of Lydia, which belonged to the Heraclids, passed to Gyges, the first known powerful Lydian ruler, in a strange way. About 700 B.C. Candaules, the Heraclid king of Lydia, boasted of his wife's beauty to Gyges, his favorite member of the palace guard. The king addressed him saying, "Gyges, as I think you do not believe me when I speak of my wife's beauty, you must contrive to see her naked." Gyges was horrified, but the king promised him that she would never know Gyges had seen her. "I will place you behind the bedroom door, from there you can watch her as she takes off her clothes and then she will give you an opportunity to look at her at your leisure. When she steps to her bed, you are at her back, you slip out without being seen." Gyges reluctantly consented and everything took place as the king had arranged, except that the queen saw Gyges as he left the bedroom. Later the queen summoned Gyges to her and said, "You have seen me naked. I submit two proposals to your choice, either kill Candaules and take possession of me and the Lydian kingdom or expect immediate death." Gyges chose to save himself. The following night the queen installed him behind the same door from which he had observed her. When the king fell asleep, Gyges killed him, taking both the queen and the kingdom. Though many citizens took up arms in the cause of their assassinated king, the Delphic oracle spoke in Gyges's favor.

Sardis: Remains of 5th Century Church East of the Temple of Artemis

As the capital of the great kingdom of Lydia, Sardis had a distinguished history marked by frequent wars. Its last king, the celebrated Croesus, was dethroned in 546 B.C. by Cyrus the Great of Persia, who made the city the western capital of the Persian Empire. In the subsequent struggle between the Greeks and Persians, Sardis remained Persian, in contrast to the Greek colonies on the coast of Asia Minor, which generally sought freedom from Persian rule. During the 499 B.C. revolt of these Ionian cities against the Persians, Sardis was sacked and destroyed by the combined Ionian and Athenian forces. In the spring of 401 B.C. Cyrus the Younger started with his forces from Sardis in his unsuccessful revolt against his brother, Artaxerxes II of Persia. This campaign is described by Xenophon in his *Anabasis*.

In 334 B.C. Sardis surrendered without battle to Alexander the Great and, in the struggle for succession

Sartmustafa: Reconstructed Gymnasium of Saıdis

among Alexander's general staff after his death in 323 B.C., it became part of the extensive territory ruled by Antigonus. In 301 B.C., when Antigonus was finally defeated and killed at Ipsus in Phrygia, northwestern Asia Minor fell to Lysimachus. In 281 B.C. all the Asian territory controlled by Lysimachus was taken over by Seleucus. Demetrius, son of Antigonus, briefly reoccupied Sardis in a desparate move against Seleucus, but he was driven from Sardis in 286 B.C. Sardis remained in the powerful Seleucid kingdom until a Roman army, commanded by Scipio Africanus, defeated Antiochus III at Magnesia in 190 B.C. and erased Seleucid power. Sardis declined under Roman influence, which was centered on Pergamum. Strabo (63 B.C. - 19 A.D.) testified to the city's decay when he wrote, "In our times, not only Sardis, but also the most famous of the other cities, were in many places seriously damaged. But the emperor (Tiberius) restored them by contributing money."

APOSTOLIC SARDIS

We must assume that the church of Sardis was established in the middle or the latter part of the 1st century. According to the Greek *Menologion*, Clement, one of the Seventy and a disciple of St. Paul (Phil. 4:3), was the first bishop of Sardis. In many ways the story of the young fellowship proved to be a repetition of the city's history. As Sardis had flourished and then decayed, so the church in Sardis flourished and then decayed. St. John admonished the Sardian Christians that they had sunk into the same decay as their once powerful city. The city's glory was in the past, and only a few Christians remained for whom there was hope. In this respect, Sardis was the opposite of Smyrna, which was decayed and yet thrived. Sardis lived and yet was dead.

"And to the angel of the church in Sardis write: 'The words of him who has the seven spirits of God and the seven stars.

" 'I know your works; you have the name of being alive, and you are dead. Awake, and strengthen what remains and is on the point of death, for I have not found your works perfect in the sight of my God. Remember then what you received and heard; keep that, and repent. If you will not awake, I will come like a thief, and you will not know at what hour I will come upon you. Yet you have still a few names in Sardis, people who have not soiled their garments; and they shall walk with me in white, for they are worthy. He who conquers shall be clad thus in white garments, and I will not blot his name out of the book of life; I will confess his name before my Father and before his angels.

Rev. 3:1-5

The similarity between the letters to the Christians in Ephesus and Sardis is striking. Degeneration was the experience in both communities, though in Ephesus it had not reached the serious proportions it had in Sardis. The Sardian church fell under the same condemnation St. Paul pronounced against the Corinthians who, after having accepted the Christian faith, had relapsed into the vices commonly practised in pagan society (I Cor. 5:10). We do not know exactly the sins of these Christians, though some had remained loyal and had not spoiled their garments. Their reward will be "white garments," which the Christians understood as symbols of the new life in the risen Lord. The symbol was a powerful one, for another "white garment," the pure white toga, was worn by Roman citizens on holidays and religious occasions. Sir William M. Ramsay points out that "there is no doubt that the great provincial festivals and shows which were celebrated in the chief Asiatic cities according to the imperial policy as a means of diffusing Roman ideas and ways were inaugurated with processions in which the Praetor was escorted to the circus as Juvenal describes it:"

What! had he seen, in his triumpant car,
Amid the dusty cirque, conspicuous far,
The Praetor perched aloft, superbly drest,
In Jove's proud tunic with a trailing west
Of Tyrian tapestry, and o'er him spread

A crown too bulky for a human head:
And now the Imperial Eagle, raised on high
With golden beak, the mark of majesty,
Trumpets before, and on the left and right
A cavalcade of nobles, all in white.

Another reward was promised also. Jesus told the Seventy to rejoice because their names were written in heaven (Luke 10:20). According to the Talmud, one heavenly book records the names of the righteous, another the names of the wicked, and a third the names of the undecided. St. John promises the faithful in Sardis that Christ Himself will confess their names before God and His angels.

HISTORICAL NOTES ON THE CHURCH IN SARDIS

We do not know the name of the bishop of Sardis at the time St. John wrote his letter to the church. In the 2nd century, Meliton, Bishop of Sardis, wrote the emperor Marcus Aurelius in defense of the Christian faith. He is the first Christian theologian to provide us with a list of the Old Testament canonical books. We know only the names of Therapon the Priest (May 27) and Apollonius (July 10) from Sardis who had laid down their lives for their Lord during the pre-Nicene persecutions but, undoubtedly, many other Sardian Christians had suffered martyrdom. Sardis was represented at the Ecumenical Council of Nicaea in 325 by its Bishop Artemidorus. In or around 400 the Goths rejected the policy of appeasement begun by the emperor Theodosius and revolted against his two sons, Arcadius and Honorius. The Goths in the east, under Gainas, plundered Sardis, causing suffering and destruction to the Christian fellowship. In 431 Maeonius of Sardis joined in the discussions of the Third Ecumenical Council in Ephesus. In 449 his successor, Florentius of Sardis, sided with the Monophysite Alexandrian party at the infamous Robber Council of Ephesus.

As the metropolis of Lydia, Sardis ranked sixth in the hierarchy of the Orthodox dioceses, and as early as the 7th century it had 27 suffragans. During the first phase of the iconoclastic controversy, which dominated political events in the Byzantine Empire throughout the 8th century, Sardis was the scene of the defeat of the first major threat to iconoclasm. Constantine V (741-775), the son of Leo III who had initiated the iconoclastic policy, was attacked by Artabasdus who, with iconodule support, managed to have himself proclaimed emperor. Constantine V, however, rallied support and attacked Artabasdus in Sardis in 743, defeating him decisively.

The bishop of Sardis, Euthymius, was a close friend of St. Theodore the Studite, the famous theologian of Constantinople, and was frequently consulted by the emperor Constantine VI and the empress Irene. During the second phase of the iconoclastic controversy he and St. Theodore the Studite were exiled. Euthymius suffered martyrdom from the wounds inflicted while in prison on December 26, 824. His successor on the episcopal throne was John I, also a friend of St. Theodore. John I also died in defense of the Orthodox cause. John II, Bishop of Sardis, attended the Council convened in 1143 by the patriarch Cosmas II Atticus which condemned the Bogomil heresy. In the middle of the 13th century Jacob Chalazas, Bishop of Sardis, ascended the patriarchal throne of Constantinople as Germanus III. A few years ago American archaeologists discovered in Sardis the ruins of a 13th century Byzantine church which had been richly decorated with painted domes, stained glass windows, and multicolored mosaics. Among the ruins they also found a reliquary with the bodily remains of a saint.

The Christian community in Sardis declined rapidly after the city was occupied by the Turks early in the 14th century. The two groups lived in separate quarters of the city, separated by walls. In 1346 Sardis was still the seat of a metropolitan, but in 1369 it did not have even a suffragan and Philadelphia became the metropolitan seat. The city still was well populated in the 14th century, but in the first years of the 15th century Tamerlane occupied Sardis and massacred — as he had in Ephesus, Magnesia, Pergamum, and Philadelphia — the population. Sardis was abandoned but the nearby village of Sart struggled on.

The location of Sardis seems never to have been forgotten. Shortly before 1670 Jean-Baptiste Tavernier "lodg'd in a Park" in Sart and recorded a brief description of the site. He recognized the Hermus Valley, Mount Tmolous, and the River Pactolus, the three geographical landmarks familiar in ancient literature, and realized that he was in Sardis, though he did not comment on the ruins. In 1671 Thomas Smith came to Sart, "a beggerly and pitiful village," and wrote a brief but interesting report on what he found. Among other things he mentioned a Christian church with several curious pillars of polished marble at the entrance, which had been converted into a mosque. The few Christians who lived there had neither a church nor a priest. Jacob Spon and George Wheler reported in 1675 that Sardis was merely a poor village with miserable huts and a large khan on the caravan route from Smyrna to Aleppo and Persia. The mosque, we are told, was a former church.

In 1698 Edmund Chishull reached the site and in his account provides a clear description of the ruins of the great Temple of Artemis. Sieur Paul Lucas passed through Sardis in 1714 but commented only briefly on the vastness and beauty of the ruins, adding that the little village is still called Sarde. The next visitor was the first archaeologist on the site, Robert Wood, famous for his monumental works on Baalbek and Palmyra. Some time before 1750 he excavated around one of the standing columns of the great Ionic temple. The first sketches of the ruins of the acropolis, the temple, and other buildings were drawn by Charles de Peyssonel. After visiting Philadelphia, Richard Chandler came to the area in 1764 and offered the most complete report up to that time. "Beyond the supposed Gerousia we turned from the road to the left, and passing the miserable village Sart, which stands with a ruinous mosque above the river, on a root or spur of the hill of the Acropolis, crossed the River Pactolus and pitched our tent in a flowery meadow." Anton von Prokesch, the famous German traveler, reached Sardis in 1825 and recorded detailed descriptions of the whole site, including the temple, acropolis, and buildings of the Roman city. One year later,

F.V.J. Arundell visited Sardis and wrote that "the foundations are fallen, her walls are thrown down. A few mud huts are inhabited by Turkish herdsmen, and a mill or two contain all the present population. The only members of the church of Sardis are two Greek servants to the Turkish miller." He noticed the ruins of two churches, one dedicated to the Holy Virgin and built with fragments of earlier edifices, the other dedicated to St. John. According to James Emerson (1829), the remnants of the Christian population, about 100 Christians and one priest, had moved to a small hamlet three miles from the ruins of Sardis. The site of Sardis appeared to him like "a smooth grassy plain, browsed over by the sheep of the peasantry or trodden by the camels of the caravans." A few years later, Charles Fellows (1838) observed, "the country over which Sardis looks is now almost deserted and the valley is become a swamp." Before the First World War the few Christians around Sardis worshipped in a small sanctuary dedicated to the Holy Virgin.

No systematic investigation of ancient Sardis had been undertaken before the arrival of the Princeton University expedition in 1910, although some attempts had been made by Spiegelthal in 1854 to examine the Lydian tombs at nearby Bin Tepé. The American archaeologists excavated the Temple of Artemis and more than 1,000 Lydian tombs.

In 1958 excavations were resumed under the direction of George M.A. Hanfmann on behalf of the American School of Oriental Research and Harvard and Cornell Universities. Among the buildings being excavated are a 2nd-7th century synagogue and a gymnasium, both of which lie immediately north of the Izmir-Ankara highway, about 200 m. east of Sartmustafa. The entrance hall and adjacent units of the gymnasium have been restored, and a number of columns in the colonnades of the palaestra have been reerected. The synagogue consists of an enormous rectangular hall almost 60 m. by 18 m. oriented east-west and ending in a broad apse 12 m. wide and 5.50 m. deep. Much of the floor mosaic remains intact, although large areas in the center of the floor are missing. In the hall is a marble slab with a menorah flanked by a *lulav* on the left and a *shofar* on the right. The composition is framed by a groove parallel to the outer edges of the slab. The building probably was destroyed by the Persian raid under Chosroes II in 615.

It is intriguing to speculate whether or not this splendid synagogue was built on the site of an older one in which the early Christians of Sardis may have assembled.

Sardis: Menorah with *shofar* and *lulav* from the Synagogue

CHRISTIAN SITES IN SARDIS

In 1912 excavations near the northeastern corner of the Temple of Artemis brought to light a small church, known as Church M, which was built when the ground level around the temple had risen one and a half meters above the temple platform. The church is nearly square with a narrow projecting apse, one doorway in the west wall and another near the west end of the north wall. A hoard of coins discovered just outside the north doorway indicate that the church was in use in the beginning of the 5th century. Immediately behind the apse is a second apse whose width

almost equals that of the church. A primitive altar, which was found *in situ* and is one of the earliest Christian altars known, is in the center of the first apse.

A 4th century three-aisled basilica known as Church E recently has been discovered about 100 m. south of the village of Sartmustafa near the road leading to the Temple of Artemis. Church E also has a second apse built east of the principal apse.

Marble Fragment from an Early Byzantine Church in Sardis
Source: Lambakes, G., *Οἱ Ἑπτὰ Ἀστέρες τῆς Ἀποκαλύψεως*, Athens, 1926

Sartmustafa: Ruins of 4th Century Church in Sardis

To the Church in Philadelphia

ON ANCIENT PHILADELPHIA

Philadelphia was founded by Attalus II of Pergamum (159-138 B.C.), whose loyalty to his brother Eumenes won him the epithet Philadelphus. Because Attalus II intended to make the city a center of Graeco-Asiatic civilization, thereby spreading the Greek language and customs to the eastern parts of Lydia and Phrygia, Philadelphia was a missionary city from its founding. In 133 B.C. it became a Roman possession. Its location made it strategically important, for the imperial post road from Rome via Troy, Pergamum, and Sardis passed through Philadelphia. The city is located on the foothills which slope gently upward from the wide valley towards the Tmolous Mountains. It was famous throughout Asia Minor for its wines, and many of its coins bore the image of Bacchus or a bacchante. After the earthquakes of 17 and 23 A.D., the emperor Tiberius aided its reconstruction. In gratitude for the imperial assistance the city changed its name to Neo-Caesarea, but the old name was restored during the reign of Nero. In approximately 20 A.D. Strabo wrote about the city, "Philadelphia is ever subject to earthquakes, incessantly the walls of the houses are cracked, different parts of the city being thus affected at different times. For this reason, but a few people lived in the city and most of them spent their lives as farmers in the country, since they have a fertile soil. Yet, one may be surprised at the few, that they are so fond of the place when their dwellings are so insecure, and one might marvel still more at those who founded the city." During the reign of Vespasian (70-79 A.D.), Philadelphia adopted another imperial name and called itself "Flavia," after the emperor's wife and daughter.

19th Century Philadelphia
Source: James M. MacDonald, *The Life and Writings of St. John.* London, 1877

APOSTOLIC PHILADELPHIA

We know very little about the beginnings of the Christian church in Philadelphia. One tradition maintains that St. Paul appointed Lucius his kinsman (Rom. 16:21) as bishop of Philadelphia but, according to the *Apostolic Constitutions*, the city's first bishop was a man named Demetrius who had been appointed by St. John.

Two churches are singled out by St. John for their faithfulness, Smyrna and Philadelphia. Both churches were poor and weak, both had suffered from the Jews, and yet, both were full of life and vigor.

> "And to the angel of the church in Philadelphia write: 'The words of the holy one, the true one, who has the key of David, who opens and no one shall shut, who shuts and no one opens.
>
> " 'I know your works. Behold, I have set before you an open door, which no one is able to shut; I know that you have but little power, and yet you have kept my word and have not denied my name. Behold, I will make those of the synagogue of Satan who say that they are Jews and are not, but lie — behold, I will make them come and bow down before your feet, and learn that I have loved you. Because you have kept my word of patient endurance, I will keep you from the hour of trial which is coming on the whole world, to try those who dwell upon earth. I am coming soon; hold fast what you have, so that no one may seize your crown. He who conquers, I will make him a pillar in the temple of my God; never shall he go out of it, and I will write on him the name of my God, and the name of the city of my God, the new Jerusalem which comes down from my God out of heaven, and my own new name. He who has an ear, let him hear what the Spirit says to the churches.'
>
> Rev. 3:7-13

Christ is the "holder of the key of David," the symbol of His authority to open and close the heavenly city, the New

Jerusalem, just as He is the holder of the keys of Death and Hades (Rev. 1:18). Well acquainted with the local situation of the Philadelphians, the author knows their weakness before the world and praises them for their loyalty under persecution and their steadfastness against the difficulties with the Jews, the "synagogue of Satan." For St. John as for St. Paul (Gal. 3:7), the true Israelites were the Christians and not the Jews. Thus, whereas in the letter to the Smyrnaeans the Christians are merely warned of the Jews, here St. John adds that Christ will make the Jews "come and bow down before your feet" or, as Martin Rist says, "the homage that the Jews had expected from others in the messianic period they now will have to pay to the Christians, which will be a sign of Christ's love for his people." The reference to the "open door" shows that the Pauline metaphor (I Cor. 16:9, II Cor. 2:12, Col. 4:3) meaning a "good opportunity" had passed into common usage in the Early Church. Philadelphia, however, was a geographic "door" as well, the gateway to the central plateau of Asia Minor. The promises extended to the faithful of the other Seven Churches are made also to the Philadelphians, who will be rewarded in their hour of trial. In addition to being assured that Christ will come "soon," each faithful Christian is promised that he will become a "pillar in the Temple," on whom Christ will write His name and that of the New Jerusalem.

HISTORICAL NOTES ON THE CHURCH IN PHILADELPHIA

About ten years after St. John wrote his letter to the Philadelphians, in approximately the year 105, the church received a letter from St. Ignatius written in Troy. In this letter St. Ignatius referred to the bishop of the church in Philadelphia by saying: "I was amazed by this gentleman, and at his ability to do more by silence than those who use vain words." He warned the congregation against the dangers of heresy and schism and admonished them to use "one eucharist." About the Judaizers he merely stated that "it is better to hear Christianity from the circumcised than Judaism from the uncircumcised." One of the distinguished Christians of this church in the 2nd century was the prophetess Ammias. In the 3rd century Philadelphia, as Thyatira, was a stronghold of the Montanist heresy, and one of the principal tenets of Montanism was that the promised New Jerusalem would descend and be established in the vicinity of Philadelphia. At the Ecumenical Council of Nicaea in 325, the church of Philadelphia was represented by Bishop Hetimasius, whose two immediate successors were Cyriacus and Theodosius. Bishop Theophanes of Philadelphia joined in the deliberations of the Council of Ephesus in 431, siding with the heretic Nestorius of Constantinople against Cyril of Alexandria.

Late in the 11th century John Ducas, to whom Laodicea had submitted, took both Philadelphia and Sardis by assault (1097) and held these cities until his revolt was put down. In 1109-1110 a Turkish expeditionary force attacked Philadelphia, but the city withstood the siege. Two years later Malik Shah, Sultan of Rum (1107-1116) tried in vain to force the city to capitulate. Fighting broke out between the Byzantine Empire and the Sultanate of Iconium in 1176, and the Byzantine emperor Manuel I Comnenus (1143-80) had to take refuge in Philadelphia after a preliminary clash with the Turkish forces. One year later, however, Sultan Kilij Arslan almost annihilated the Byzantine army at Myriocephalon, a defeat as serious a setback for the Byzantines as that at Mantzikert in 1071.

During this period the power of the Byzantine landed aristocracy was increasingly detrimental to the power of the central state. When Manuel I Comnenus died he was succeeded by his underage son, Alexius II Comnenus, and the regency was unable to maintain control. Andronicus I Comnenus (1183-1185), an opponent of the feudal aristocracy, grabbed the reins of power for two years, but when he was deposed he was succeeded by Isaac II Angelus (1185-95) of the powerful Angeli family from Philadelphia. This family provided three emperors to Byzantium but only the first was able to help the disintegrating state. Even Isaac

118

II Angelus, however, could not stop the advance of the almost openly hostile Crusading forces under the German emperor Frederick I Barbarossa (ca. 1123-1190) through Byzantine territory. Frederick I spent two days in Philadelphia before continuing south through Laodicea. Philadelphia remained a major center of Byzantine feudal power even after the fall of Constantinople to the forces of the Fourth Crusade in 1204. One of the first tasks Theodore I Lascaris (1204-22) had to do in reconstructing the Byzantine Empire was to control Theodore Mancaphas, who had established himself as an independent ruler in Philadelphia. Theodore I brought Philadelphia under the control of the Byzantine Empire of Nicaea, but Mancaphas escaped to the court of the sultan of Iconium.

Despite repeated attacks from the growing Ottoman state, Philadelphia remained in Byzantine hands until the end of the 14th century. In 1304 a Turkish siege of the city was broken by the Catalan Grand Company. After the Serbians, the only Balkan force from which the declining Byzantine state could seek aid, were defeated by the Ottomans at the Maritsa River in 1371, John V Palaeologus (1341-91) was forced to become a vassal of the Ottoman sultan. Manuel II, the loyal son of John V, was forced to live in the sultan's court, and both father and son had to supply Byzantine troops and accompany the sultan on campaign. In this humiliating role Manuel aided Bayazid's capture of Philadelphia, the last Byzantine city of Asia Minor, in 1390.

It was a remarkable feat for Philadelphia to have retained its independence from the surrounding Turks for so long, and it follows that the apostolic church here was the strongest of the Seven Churches. It was the home of the famous mid-14th century Byzantine hymnographer and orator, Theoleptus, and of the theologian and bishop, Macarius II Chrysocephalus, known for his New Testament homilies and exegetical works. In 1347 Macarius II was made responsible for the sees of Smyrna and Phocaea in addition to Philadelphia, making Philadelphia one of the principal dioceses in Asia Minor and leading the metropolitan to sign the synodal decrees with the impressive title: "Metropolitan of Philadelphia, Hypertimus and Exarch of all Lydia and Universal Judge of the Romans." In 1385 Philadelphia was given control also of the churches of Synnada and Hierapolis.

Following the devastation of Asia Minor by Tamerlane in the first few years of the 15th century, many Christians fled to Venice, where a colony of 4,000 Greeks settled. In 1578, the patriarch of Constantinople sent Gabriel Severus as exarch to Venice with the title of Metropolitan of Philadelphia. The last exarch and metropolitan of Philadelphia was Miletius of Tipalda in the beginning of the 18th century.

In 1671 Thomas Smith visited Alashehir, the Turkish name for Philadelphia and meaning the reddish city, and remarked that "it was a city of as great strength as beauty, having three strong walls towards the plain, a great part of the innermost wall was still standing, though decayed and broken down in several places." Smith found that the Church of St. John, probably the former cathedral, had been turned into a dump for the offal of slaughtered beasts. He further reported that other churches had been converted into mosques and that only four churches survived. Paul Rycaut, however, visiting Alashehir a few years later, mentioned twelve churches in the city. The church in Philadelphia continued to have martyrs. In the middle of the 17th century, Demetrius of Philadelphia, although the son of a priest, had embraced Islam but returned to his faith and suffered martyrdom (June 2). One century later a Philadelphia Christian named Hadji-George moved from Alashehir to Karacasu where he became a Muslim, but he later publicly confessed his former faith and was executed (October 2).

Dr. James Griffiths passed through Alashehir in 1785 and was impressed by the local skill in dyeing, which he considered superior to any other place in the country. No ruins of the ancient city were visible, but he noticed seven or eight active churches. In 1826 the Greek bishop of Philadelphia told the Reverend F.V.J. Arundell that the city had 3,000 Turkish families and 300 Greek families. The bishop also said that there were twenty-five churches remaining but only five in use. Arundell saw the ruins of the Church of St. John, consisting of "a high stone wall having the remains of a brick arch on the top." James Emerson entered Alashehir three years later and was full of praise for the city "which still survives, while all her sister cities had crumbled into decay. The remnants of her Christian temples rise amidst the waving olive-groves." He estimated the number of Christians to be between one and two thousand, chiefly Turkish speaking. Gotthilf von Schubert (1836) was told that no more than fifty Greek families lived in the city.

The so-called wall of skulls or bones is repeatedly mentioned by travelers from the 17th century onwards. About one mile west of the city travelers as late as the 19th century reported seeing a portion of the wall believed to have been built by the Ottoman sultan Bayazid with the bones of the Christian community, which he massacred while they were worshiping in a nearby church dedicated to St. John.

Though declining in numbers, the Christian community in Alashehir remained proud of its apostolic origins. The Reverend H. Christmas, visiting in 1851, was shown the "very old church, some of whose high and strong walls are still standing, on one of which may be perceived the image of St. John the Evangelist." In 1860 A.S. Noroff listed the following five active churches: St. George (the metropolitan church), the Nativity of the Virgin, St. Theodore, St. Michael, St. Marina. The churches of St. John the Theologian and Naum the Prophet were in ruins. There have been no Christians living in Alashehir since 1922.

CHRISTIAN RUINS IN PHILADELPHIA

In 1973 Alashehir had 20,300 inhabitants, and those asked by the author all were aware of the city's distinguished history. With considerable pride, many people in Alashehir claimed, correctly, that their city was one of the oldest towns bearing the name of "brotherly love." In the summer of 1973 a civic delegation from the Italian town of Filadelfia in the province of Catanzaro visited Alashehir and offered prayers in the ruins of the Christian basilica, traditionally identified as

122

the Church of St. John the Theologian.

The ruins of the Christian basilica, built of red brick and still retaining some remains of 11th century frescoes, are on Ismet Pasha Street, opposite the new Bayazid I Çamii in the Besh Eylul district. According to local tradition this building served as the cathedral and was dedicated to St. John the Theologian. The entrance to the ruins is locked, but the keys are available at the Alashehir police station.

In addition to Alashehir, there used to be a Philadelphia in Cilicia-Isauria, near the modern Sari Kavak. Around 1900 a number of Egyptian papyri were discovered in the ancient Roman village of Philadelphia in the Fayyum Oasis of Egypt. Today this village is known as Kom al-Kharaba al-Kebir. One of the cities of the Palestinian Decapolis was known as Philadelphia, today Amman and the capital of the Hashemite Kingdom of Jordan. The south Italian town of Filadelfia is between Naples and Reggio and, finally, there is Philadelphia in Pennsylvania, the Philadelphia of William Penn.

Marble Fragment from an Early Byzantine Church in Philadelphia
Source: Lambakes, G., Οἱ Ἑπτὰ Ἀστέρες τῆς Ἀποκαλύψεως, Athens, 1926

Alashehir: Ruins of Byzantine Church of Philadelphia

123

To the Church in Laodicea

ON ANCIENT LAODICEA

Antiochus II (261-246 B.C.) rebuilt and renamed the city, originally called Diospolis and Rhoas, after his sister-wife Laodice sometime between the beginning of his reign and his divorce from her in 253 B.C. In 188 B.C. the whole region of Laodicea became part of the kingdom of Pergamum and in 129 B.C. it was included in the Roman province of Asia. In addition to being on a fertile plain, excellent sheep, according to Strabo, were raised in the surrounding country, good "not only for the softness of their wool, but also for its ravenblack color." The geographical position was also favorable for the city, for Laodicea was a fortress city on the great eastern highway through the Lycus Valley, the most frequented trade route from the interior to the west. The road from Pergamum through the Hermus Valley to Pisidia and Pamphylia also passed through Laodicea, and roads from eastern Caria and from central and western Phrygia converged here.

The Romans made Laodicea a free city, and by the end of the 1st century B.C. it was one of the largest cities of Asia Minor. Strabo informs us that "though formerly small, it grew large in our time and in that of our fathers, even though it has been damaged by the siege of Mithradates Eupator (ca. 111-63 B.C.)." The principal deity worshipped in Laodicea was the Phrygian god Men Karou, the Carian Men. In connection with this god's temple there grew up a famous school of medicine, which followed the teachings of Herophilus (330-250 B.C.) who began administering compound mixtures to his patients on the principle that compound diseases require compound medicines. Two skeptic philosophers, Antiochus and Theiodas, were born in Laodicea.

Laodicea: Theater, with the "Tepid Springs" of Hierapolis (Pamukkale) in the Background

During the 1st century B.C. there was a flourishing colony of Jews in Laodicea. Their freedom of worship was guaranteed by the city fathers. The Laodicean Jews sent gold to Jerusalem annually, though at least once, in 62 B.C., the Romans confiscated the money for the city treasury.

APOSTOLIC LAODICEA

The Christian faith was introduced into Laodicea during St. Paul's ministry in Asia Minor. The church was founded by Epaphras of nearby Colossae, who shared the care of the young community with Nympha, in whose house the congregation assembled (Col. 4:13, 15). As Edgar J. Goodspeed has suggested, it is possible that St. Paul addressed his Letter to Philemon to the church in Laodicea wishing it also to be read to the Colossians. Sir William M. Ramsay published an inscription from Laodicea mentioning a certain Marcus Sestius Philemon. While it would be fanciful to identify this person with the Biblical Philemon, it is nevertheless clear that the city had at least one prominent

Laodicea: Gymnasium

citizen of this name. An apocryphal letter purporting to be by St. Paul to the Laodiceans is extant in a 6th century manuscript written for Victor of Capua, a transparent attempt to supply the lost letter by the Apostle. This apocryphal letter, mentioned by various writers, notably Gregory the Great, from the 4th century onwards consists of twenty short lines and reflects material from St. Paul's Letter to the Philippians and other Pauline letters. Though enjoying certain respect in the Middle Ages, it already had been condemned by St. Jerome (348-420).

We must assume that Archippus (Nov. 2), whom St. Paul advised "see that you fulfil the ministry which you have received in the Lord" (Col. 4:17), was no longer head of the Laodicean community when St. John addressed his letter to this church. According to the *Apostolic Constitutions*, Archippus was followed by Nymphas as Bishop of Laodicea.

> "And to the angel of the church in Laodicea write: 'The words of the Amen, the faithful and true witness, the beginning of God's creation.
>
> " 'I know your works; you are neither cold nor hot. Would that you were cold or hot! So, because you are lukewarm, and neither cold nor hot, I will spew you out of my mouth. For you say, I am rich, I have prospered, and I need nothing; not knowing that you are wretched, pitiable, poor, blind, and naked. Therefore I counsel you to buy from me gold refined by fire, that you may be rich, and white garments to clothe you and to keep the shame of your nakedness from being seen, and salve to anoint your eyes, that you may see. Those whom I love, I reprove and chasten; so be zealous and repent. Behold, I stand at the door and knock; if any one hears my voice and opens the door, I will come in to him and eat with him, and he with me. He who conquers, I will grant him to sit with me on my throne, as I myself conquered and sat down with my Father on his throne. He who has an ear, let him hear what the Spirit says to the churches.' "

Rev. 3:14-22

Laodicea was the seventh city to which the Johannine letters were addressed. Since the church in Laodicea was unable to reject the temptations and attractions of the world, it shall be rejected by the Lord. The references to the cold, hot, and tepid waters are especially relevant since none of the other cities were as dependent upon an external water supply as Laodicea; an aqueduct brought water from springs about six miles to the south. If the aqueduct were cut, the city was helpless, which must have prevented the citizens from ever feeling secure when threatened with attack. Using the metaphor of the water, St. John reminds the Laodiceans that there was no compromise between absolute loyalty to Christ and participation in the imperial cults.

St. John's reference to the church of Laodicea as being lukewarm is interesting because of the nearby tepid waters of Hierapolis, modern Pamukkale or "cotton tower." Pamukkale, situated on a plateau formed by lime deposits of a stream rushing from a spring in the nearby hills, is about six miles from Laodicea. From the ruins of Laodicea the hill indeed resembles a giant pile of cotton. Today Pamukkale is one of the principal tourist attractions of western Turkey, and several large pools invite visitors to enjoy the 95° water. The water contains calcium carbonate, sulphur, chlorine, and traces of sodium, iron, and magnesium. In the crystalline waters of the spring one can clearly see the columns and column capitals of ancient Hierapolis. Obviously, St. John knew the tepid springs of Hierapolis, which provided him with the imagery to describe the lack of spirituality and commitment of the Laodicean Christians.

Alluding to the wealth of some of its citizens, St. John contrasted wordly riches of Laodicea with spiritual wealth from Christ, a "gold refined by fire," the fire of persecution, and spoke of the "white garments" in which martyrs would be clothed. Just as God reproves those whom He loves, so Christ chastens His beloved Laodiceans, urging them to be zealous and repent of their lukewarmness and complacency.

Those who listen and repent are invited to participate in

128

the messianic banquet, a feast enjoyed by the righteous in the presence of Christ. In the Gospels, Jesus repeatedly referred to this messianic banquet which He would celebrate with His disciples in the Heavenly Kingdom (Mark 14:25, Luke 12:36). Those Laodiceans who remain faithful are promised that they will sit with Christ on His throne, and the promise that the martyrs will rule finds its fulfilment in the millenial reign with Christ (Rev. 20:4).

HISTORICAL NOTES ON THE CHURCH IN LAODICEA

The church of Laodicea suffered as much as the other churches of Asia Minor from the persecutions of the 2nd to the 4th century. In the latter part of the 2nd century, Sagaris, Bishop of Laodicea, suffered martyrdom and was buried in Laodicea. From the life of St. Sisinius, Bishop of Laodicea, we learn that in the 2nd century the church was five stadia outside the city walls. When the bishop and Artemon the presbyter of Laodicea destroyed the images in the temples of Diana and Apollo they were arrested, and Artemon would have suffered martyrdom had not Sisinius healed the Roman centurion Patricius, who then embraced the Christian faith. Later, however, Patricius apostatized and Artemon, refusing to worship the idols, was killed for his faith. Eugenius occupied the episcopal throne of Laodicea during the first few years of the reign of Constantine the Great, and he is credited with constructing a large and beautiful church adorned with wall paintings and wood carvings. Bishop Nunechius represented the see of Laodicea at the Ecumenical Council of Nicaea in 325 which condemned the Arians as heretics, but Nunechius's successor Cecropius was an Arian who consequently was transferred by the emperor to Nicomedia. He was succeeded by Nonnius.

In 367 Laodicea was the site of the Fourth Synod, which issued forty disciplinary canons dealing with such matters as the prohibition of usury and the use of holy places by heretics. The Fourth Synod also ruled that digamists were to be held blameless, that no one should marry heretics, that the clergy should not enter taverns, and that beds should not be set up in churches. Other canons prohibited mixed bathing and the solemnization of marriages during Lent.

Bishop Aristonicus represented the church of Laodicea at the Third Ecumenical Council in Ephesus in 431. Bishop Nunechius II of Laodicea participated in the Robber Council of Ephesus in 449 and the Fourth Ecumenical Council in Chalcedon in 451. Laodicea continued to be prosperous well into the 5th century, but was shattered by a devastating earthquake in 494.

In 1094 the city was severely damaged when captured by the Selçuks and made part of the Sultanate of Rum. Three years later Byzantine troops commanded by John Ducas recaptured Laodicea. Ducas garrisoned troops in Sardis and Philadelphia, but did not do so in Laodicea. Between 1092 and 1110 the city was sacked repeatedly by the Turks. In 1120 Emperor John Comnenus (1118-1143) rebuilt Laodicea, but a few years later the Christian population began to leave the city, especially in view of the massacre of many of its citizens including its Bishop Solomon in 1161.

Late in the 12th century the Christians built a new city also called Laodicea, on the site of modern Denizli, for it is described as being located at the foot of a very lofty mountain, which would be true of Denizli, but not of the old Laodicea. In 1190, the German emperor Frederick I Barbarossa entered Laodicea on his ill fated way towards Jerusalem on the Third Crusade. He was received so kindly that he prayed on his knees for the prosperity of the people. A few years later, however, the whole region was dreadfully ravaged by the Turks. During the Mongol incursion of the 13th century the sultan gave Laodicea to the Byzantines, but they were unable to defend it, and thus it returned to the Turks.

In the 14th century the declining economy of the metropolitan see of Laodicea was aided by placing the patriarchal possessions of Coula, Coulida, Chonae (Colossae), and Cotyaeum under its administration. By 1394, however, Laodicea was deprived of all of these assets except for Chonae. In 1332, the famous Arab traveler, Ibn Batuta of

Tangier, visited Laodicea. The approach to the city was made dangerous by robbers, who controlled the town of Cotyaeum. Once in the city, Ibn Batuta wrote of the "splendid gardens, perennial streams, and gushing springs. Its bazaars are very fine and in them are manufactured cotton fabrics edged with gold embroidery, unequalled in their kind. Most of the artisans there are Greek women, who are subject to the Muslims and who pay dues to the sultan, including the jizya." Ibn Batuta also comments that the men of Laodicea "buy beautiful Greek slave girls and put them out to prostitution, and each girl has to pay a regular due to her master. The girls go into the bath houses along with the men . . . " By the 15th century Laodicea had degenerated to become a small village. The last bishop of Laodicea of whom we have a record was named Theophylact. He participated in the Council of Constantinople in 1450 which condemned the decisions of the Ecumenical Council of Ferrara (1438) and Florence (1439).

In the latter part of the 17th century, when the Reverend Thomas Smith visited ancient Laodicea, the site was referred to by the Turks as "Eski Hisar," meaning "Old Castle." It was inhabited only by wolves, jackals, and foxes. A century later, Richard Chandler (1764) and his party were almost killed by robbers between Denizli and the ruins of Laodicea. The first ruin Chandler saw was the amphitheater, a hollow area about 1,000 feet wide, with many seats remaining. At its western end he identified the vaulted passage as a stable "designed for horses and chariots." He visited the odeum with seats remaining in the side of the hill, and beyond the odeum he saw some marble arches standing, the ruins of a gymnasium. "No traces of houses, churches or mosques, all was silence and solitude."

The 19th century travelers — James Emerson (1829), Hamilton (1836), Charles Fellows (1838), A.S. Noroff (1860) — give similar reports. "No wretched outcast dwells in the midst of it, it has long been abandoned to the owl and to the fox," indeed, "nothing can exceed the desolation and melancholy appearance of the site of Laodicea." "All that we saw were the bones of a camel picked neatly clean." A few years later the ruins of Laodicea served as a quarry for the inhabitants of the nearby villages.

In 1961-63 the Nymphaeum in ancient Laodicea was excavated by archaeologists from Laval University in Quebec, Canada, under the direction of Jean des Gagniers.

The ruins of Laodicea easily can be reached from Denizli by following the main road to Pamukkale (Hierapolis). At the Tugla Kiremit factory a road sign shows the way to the village of Eskihisar and the ruins of Laodicea, which are on a flat-topped hill between the villages of Eskihisar and Goncale. Some traces of the ancient city wall remain. At the southern end of the plateau is the amphitheater or stadium, dedicated by a wealthy citizen to the emperor Vespasian. It was used both for athletic and gladiatorial shows. The remains of the large building east of the stadium is a gymnasium dedicated to the emperor Hadrian. The city had two theaters, one on the northeastern slope of the plateau, the other facing northwest. There was also a small odeum. In the center of the city was the nymphaium, built early in the 3rd century during the reign of the emperor Caracalla. Remains of an aqueduct, which carried water from the upper part of the present town of Denizli to Laodicea, can still be seen. As one of the 19th century travelers remarked, "in the summer the whole area of the ancient city, once so gay and populous, swarms with myriads of snakes, which make it dangerous for any person to ramble about the ruins; and at other seasons with wolves and foxes."

> I know your works; you are neither cold nor hot.
> Would that you were cold or hot! So, because you are lukewarm, and neither cold or hot, I will spew you out of my mouth.

CHRISTIAN RUINS IN LAODICEA

Extensive excavations certainly would unearth several churches in the area of Laodicea. The sites of two former churches have been suggested, one near the so-called Syrian

Gate, the other north of the nymphaium. During the excavations of the nymphaium several marble slabs with cross designs were found; they could date from the 5th or 6th century. In fact, part of the nymphaium, what is known as niche C, was used as a church.

Laodicea: Marble Fragments from a 5th Century Church
Nymphaeum

EPILOGUE

The traveler to the Seven Churches in Asia Minor will see clearly that the prophetic revelations concerning these churches by the Seer of Patmos have been fulfilled. Yet, there is another dimenison to this story, for in addition to the developments we have traced through the ages, the language of the Apocalypse sharpens as we approach the third millenium. Today, not merely individual congregations but whole cultures and ways of life are being challenged, and the relevance of these letters cannot be exaggerated by the student of history. As in the 1st century, communities are undergoing rapid social changes which may either lead to their decay and death or to their growth in maturity and strength.

Are we like the Ephesians? Yes, St. John knew Ephesus as a "city of changes." Change is the order of life, though everything depends upon the way we are changing. Like the Ephesians we have fallen and the call to repentance is as urgent today as 1900 years ago. Are we like the Smyrnaeans? Yes, though poor in this world's possessions, we can, nevertheless, be rich in the values of the spiritual life, and like the Smyrnaeans we are called to be faithful to God and man in our daily affairs. Are we like the Pergamenes? Yes, we too dwell near Satan's throne, tempted to exchange our faithfulness to God for all kinds of loyalties that happen to demand our attention, and only a few of us have held fast His name and not denied the faith. Are we like the Thyatirans? Yes, we are confronted with as many spurious beliefs and esoteric cults tempting us to seek superior forms of knowledge as the Thyatirans of old. Are we like the Sardians? Yes, we cherish a glorious spiritual past, but many are

Patmos: Bell Tower of the Monastery of St. John

spiritually dead and have defiled their garments. Are we like the Philadelphians? Yes, I sincerely hope that we recognize the open door which no one is able to shut, and which always provides new opportunities of service. Are we like the Laodiceans? I regret to say that we are lukewarm. We have not rejected the Message outright, but we do not fully accept it either. We claim wealth and prosperity which has led to false pride and arrogance.

The Seven Letters are a suitable mirror of our personal and collective predicaments, and their lessons are as pertinent to our days as to the 1st century churches of Asia Minor. "He who has an ear, let him hear what the Spirit says to the Churches" (Rev. 3:22).

The Travelers Cited in the Text

1412-1431	Cyriacus of Ancona
1573-1589	Reinhold Lubenau
1610	George Sandys
1621	Sieur Louis Deshayes de Courmesnin
1622	P. Pacifique
1630	Jean Baptiste Tavernier
1655	Jean Thevenot
1665	Robert de Dreux
1671	Thomas Smith
1674	Corneille le Brun
1675	Jacob Spon and George Wheler
1677	Joseph Georgirenes
1661-1678	Paul Rycaut
1688	O. Dapper
1689	Edmund Chishull
1700-1702	Pitton de Tournefort
1711	M. Eneman
1714	Paul Lucas
1731	Basil G. Barsky
1738-1739	John Montague, fourth earl of Sandwich
1739	Richard Pococke
1750	Robert Wood
1759	J. Aegidius van Egmont
1764	Richard Chandler
1778-1780	C.S. Sonnini
1785	James Griffiths
1797	James Dallaway
1802	Edward Daniel Clarke
1809-1810	John Cam Hobhouse
1817	H. Lindsay
1818-1820	John Fuller
1824-1825	Anton von Prokesch
1826-1833	F.V.J. Arundell
1829	James Emerson
1836-1837	William J. Hamilton

1836-1837	Gotthilf Heinrich von Schubert
1838	Charles G. Addison
1838	Charles Fellows
1844	Konstantin von Tischendorf
1850	H. Christmas
1853-1854	C.T. Newton
1860	A.S. Noroff
1874	Henry Fanshawe Tozer
1884-1885	Karl Krumbacher
1888	J. Theodore Bent

Bibliography

Addison, Charles G., *Damascus and Palmyra*. London, 1838.

Akurgal, Ekrem, *Ancient Civilizations and Ruins in Turkey*. Istanbul, 1970.

Alzinger, Wilhelm, *Die Stadt des siebten Weltwunders*. Wien, 1962.

Arundell, F.V.J., *A Visit to the Seven Churches of Asia with an Excursion into Pisidia*. London, 1828.

Banks, Florence Aiken, *Coins of Bible Days*. New York, 1955.

Barklay, William, *Letters to the Seven Churches*. Nashville, Tenn., 1957.

Bean, George E., *Aegean Turkey*. London, 1966.

———, *Turkey Beyond the Meander*. London, 1971.

Bent, J. Theodore, "What St. John saw on Patmos," *The Nineteenth Century*, XXIV, 1888, pp. 813-821.

Bird, S.W.H., *And Unto Smyrna. The Story of a Church in Asia Minor*. London, 1956.

Bournis, Theodoritos, *I Was in the Isle of Patmos*. Athens, 1968.

Butler, Howard Crosby, *Sardis. The Excavations 1910-1914*. London, 1922.

Cadoux, Cecil John, *Ancient Smyrna. A History of the City from the earliest times to 324 A.D.* Oxford, 1938.

Camus, E. le, *Voyage aux Sept Eglises de l'Apocalypse*. Paris, 1896.

Chandler, Richard, *Travels in Asia Minor or an Account of a Tour made at the expense of the Society of Dilettanti*. Oxford, 1775.

Chishull, Edmund, *Travels in Turkey and back to England*. London, 1747.

Christmas, H., *The Shores and Islands of the Mediterranean, including a visit to the Seven Churches of Asia*. London, 1851.

Clarke, Edward D., *Travels in various countries*. Cambridge, 1810-1823.

Dallaway, James, *Constantinople Ancient and Modern*. London, 1797.

Dapper, O., *Description exacte des isles de l'Archipel*. Amsterdam, 1703.

De Dreux, Robert, *Voyage en Turquie et en Grèce*. Paris, 1925.

Deissmann, Adolf, "Zur Ephesischen Gefangenschaft des Apostel Paulus," *Anatolian Studies*, 1923, pp. 121-127.

De Peyssonel, Charles, *Observations historiques et géographiques sur les peuples barbares*. Paris, 1765.

Deutsch, Bernard, F., *Our Lady of Ephesus*. Milwaukee, 1965.

Emerson, James, *Letters from the Aegean*. London, 1829.

Eneman, M., *Resa i Orienten 1711-1712*. Upsala, 1898.

Eusebius Pamphilus, *The Ecclesiastical History*.

Fellows, Charles, *A Journal written during an excursion in Asia Minor*. London, 1839.

Flynn, Vernon P., *The Seven Churches Today*. Istanbul, 1963.

Forschungen in Ephesos, "Die Marienkirche in Ephesos" (IV, 1, Wien, 1932); "Das Cömeterium der Sieben Schläfer" (IV, 2, Wien, 1937); "Die Johanniskirche" (IV, 3, Wien, 1951).

Fuller, John, *Narrative of a Tour through some parts of the Turkish Empire*. London, 1830.

Gagniers, Jean des, *Laodicée du Lycos*. Paris, 1969.

Georgirenes, Joseph, *A description of the present state of Samos, Nicaria, Patmos and Mount Athos*. London, 1678.

Goodenough, Erwin R., *Jewish Symbols in the Graeco-Roman Period*. New York, 1953.

Goodspeed, Edgard J., *An Introduction to the New Testament*. Chicago, 1937.

142

Griffiths, J., *Travels in Europe, Asia Minor and Arabia*. London, 1805.

Hobhouse, J.C., *A Journey through Albania and other Provinces of Turkey in Europe and Asia*. London, 1813.

Ignatius of Antioch, *Letter to the Ephesians*. *Letter to the Philadelphians*. *Letter to the Smyrnaeans*.

James, Montague R., *The Apocryphal New Testament*. Oxford, 1924.

Johnson, Shermane, "Laodicea and its Neighbours," *Biblical Archaeologist*, XIII, 1950, 1-18.

Krumbacher, Karl, *Griechische Reise*. Berlin, 1886.

Lambakes, G. Οἱ Ἑπτὰ Ἀστέρες τῆς Ἀποκαλύψεως, Athens, 1926.

Lohmeyer, Ernst, *Die Offenbarung des Johannes*. Tübingen, 1926.

Michaelis, Wilhelm, "Das Gefängnis des Paulus in Ephesus," *Byzantinisch-Neugriechische Jahrbücher*, VI, 1927-1928, pp. 1-18.

Musurillo, Herbert, *The Acts of the Christian Martyrs*. Oxford, 1972.

Newton, C.T., *Travels and Discources in the Levant*. London, 1865.

Nicol, Donald M., "Philadelphia and the Tagaris Family," *Neo-Hellenika*, 1, 1970, pp. 7-17.

Noroff, A.S., *Die Sieben Kirchen der Offenbarung St. Johannis*. Leipzig, 1860.

Oeconomos, Lysimachos, *The Tragedy of the Christian Near East*. London, 1923.

Ostrogorsky, George, *History of the Byzantine State*. Oxford, 1968.

Papadopoulos, St. A., *Patmos Guide for the visitor*. Athens, 1967.

————, *The Monastery of St. John the Theologian in Patmos*, Athens, 1969.

Pococke, Richard, *A Description of the East*. London, 1743-1745.

Prokesch, Anton von, *Erinnerungen aus Aegypten und Kleinasien*. Wien, 1831.

Ramsay, W.M., *The Cities and Bishoprics of Phrygia*. Oxford, 1895.

————, *The Letters to the Seven Churches of Asia and their place in the plan of the Apocalypse*. London, 1909.

Rist, Martin, "The Revelation of St. John the Divine," *The Interpreter's* Bible, XII.

Rolleston, George, *Report on Smyrna*. London, 1856.

Rycaut, Paul, *The Present State of the Greek and Armenian Churches, Anno Christi 1678*. London, 1679.

Sahm, W., *Beschreibung der Reisen des Reinhold Lubenau*. Königsberg, 1912.

Sandwich, Earl of, *A Voyage performed by the late Earl of Sandwich in the years 1738 and 1799*. London, 1799.

Schubert, Gotthilf H. von, *Reise in das Morgenland in den Jahren 1836 und 1837*. Erlangen, 1840.

Smith, Thomas, *Remarks upon the Manners etc. of the Turks together with a Survey of the Seven Churches of Asia as they now ly in Ruines*. London, 1678.

Sonnini, C.S., *Voyage en Grèce et en Turquie*. Paris, 1801.

Spon, Jacob, and Wheler, George, *Morgenländische Reise samt der Beschreibung der Sieben Kirchen derer in der Offenbarung Johannis Meldung geschieht*. Nürnberg, 1690.

Stauffer, Ethelbert, *Christ and the Caesars*. Philadelphia, 1955.

Strabo, *Geography*, V & VI.

Sukenik, E., *Ancient Synagogues in Palestine and Greece*. London, 1934.

Tcherikover, Victor, *Hellenistic Civilization and the Jews.* Philadelphia, 1959.

Tischendorf, Konstantin V., *Travels in the East.* London, 1847.

Tournefort, M., *A Voyage into the Levant.* London, 1718.

Tozer, Henry F., *The Islands of the Aegean.* Oxford, 1890.

Van Egmont, J. Aegidius and John Heyman, *Travels through part of Europe, Asia Minor, etc.* London, 1759.

Vryonis, Speros, *The Decline of Medieval Hellenism in Asia Minor and the Process of Islamization from the Eleventh through the Fifteenth Century.* London, 1971.

Wood, Robert, *The Ruins of Palmyra, otherwise Tedmor in the Desert.* London, 1753.

INDEX

150

153

154

Wood, R., 109

Xanthos, E., 15
Xenophon, 79, 104
Xerxes, 33

Zakinthos, 14
Zebedee, 4
Zeus, 34, 80, 82, 88, 91, 94
Zeus Soter, 80, 82

In the Footsteps of the Saints
A new series of travel guides

Otto F.A. Meinardus

A new series of inexpensive guides for travellers and others interested in retracing the journeys of early Christian figures. The geographical context of the lands described is supplemented · by historical accounts, references to recent archaeological finds and observation about the life and customs of the inhabitants.

Each title is about 160 pages and is available in either a paperback or hardback version; the text is illustrated by many photographs. All books are uniform in format, 5½" x 8¼".
PRICE: $4.95 (paperback)
$7.50 (hardcover)

ST. PAUL IN EPHESUS and the Cities of Galatia and Cyprus
ISBN 0-89241-044-2 (paperback)
0-89241-071-x (hardcover)

ST. PAUL IN GREECE
ISBN 0-89241-045-0 (paperback)
0-89241-072-8 (hardcover)

ST. PAUL'S LAST JOURNEY
ISBN 0-89241-046-9 (paperback)
0-89241-073-6 (hardcover)

ST. JOHN OF PATMOS and the Seve Churches of the Apocalypse.
ISBN 0-89241-043-4 (paperback)
0-89241-070-1 (hardcover)

CARATZAS BROTHERS, PUBLISHERS
246 Pelham Road
New Rochelle, New York 10805